Emil Loriks

Builder of a New

Economic Order

by

Elizabeth E. Williams

Center for Western Studies
Sioux Falls, South Dakota
1987

F
656
.L6
W5
1987

Published by
THE CENTER FOR WESTERN STUDIES
A
HISTORICAL RESEARCH AND ARCHIVAL
Agency of
Augustana College
Sioux Falls,
South Dakota

ISBN 0-931170-39-7 Softcover
      0-931170-38-9 Hardcover
Library of Congress Catalog Number 87-71835
First Edition
Printed by Crescent Publishing, Inc., Hills, Minnesota
Manufactured in the United States of America

The Center for Western Studies is a cultural museum and a study and research agency of Augustana College, Sioux Falls, South Dakota, concerned principally with South Dakota and the adjoining states, the Prairie Plains, and with certain aspects of the Great Plains and the Trans-Mississippi West.

The Center serves as a resource for teachers, research scholars, students and the general public, through which studies, research projects and related activities are initiated and conducted, and by which assistance can be provided to interested individuals and groups. Its goal is to provide awareness of the multi-faceted culture of this area, with special emphasis on Dakota (Sioux) Indian Culture.

The Center was founded in the conviction that this region possesses a unique and important heritage which should not be lost or forgotten. Consequently, the Center for Western Studies seeks to provide services to assist researchers in their study of the region, to promote a public consciousness of the importance of preserving cultural and historical resources, to collect published and unpublished materials, art and artifacts, important to the understanding of the region, and to undertake and sponsor projects, to sponsor conferences and provide permanent displays and shows which reflect the art and culture of the West, particularly the Sioux.

The Center maintains an archive and possesses one of the finest collections available of books relating to all aspects of the American West. The Center continually seeks to expand its collections in order to provide maximum assistance to interested scholars, students at all levels, and the general public. The collections include excellent representative Sioux Indian art, bead and quill work, western art consisting of original oils, water colors, bronzes, photographs, and steel engravings.

To my late father,
A.D. Evenson,

who first encouraged me to write

Table of Contents

Acknowledgments

Many institutions and individuals have nurtured this book throughout its development. Credit, first of all, goes to the South Dakota Committee on the Humanities, and its executive director, John W. Whalen, for its support, beginning with the two research grants about Emil Loriks, and for its support of the book's publication. Other major funding sources for publication include the South Dakota Farmers Union, in particular, Leland Swanson, Norman Tofflemire and Charles Groth; Harvest State Cooperatives, Allen Hanson, president (formerly Grain Terminal Association) whose foundation supported this project; GTA Feeds of Sioux Falls, Allan Walker and Stephen Simons, which helped to support the initial research and the two public meetings about Emil Loriks; and the Loriks-Peterson Museum Society of Oldham, Verna Lee, president, which supported the book both financially and with the museum resources in Oldham.

The Center for Western Studies at Augustana College in Sioux Falls has been most supportive from the time the writer first suggested her idea for a book about Emil Loriks to director Dr. Sven G. Froiland through the entire publication process. Acknowledgment is also expressed to Wayne Petersen of CWS for his financial administration.

The South Dakota State University Department of Speech, headed by Dr. Judith Zivanovic, was administratively responsible for the two research grants. Dr. Wayne E. Hoogestraat of the Department of Speech was the author's thesis advisor for her study of Emil Loriks' Farmers Union speeches, and Dr. Mike Schliessmann of the Department has provided continued encouragement and thoughtful criticism of various papers resulting from the ongoing study. Throughout the Loriks research and writing process, Departmental Secretary Ila Asmus has functioned as a most competent and willing typist and word processor.

The Loriks papers were initially inventoried by Dr. Larry Roberts, formerly of the South Dakota State University History Department. This inventory provided an invaluable road map for the author's extended travels through the papers.

At the time research was in progress, the Loriks papers were housed at the American State Bank in Oldham; appreciation is expressed to Francis Malone and all the other bank personnel who were so cooperative.

Invaluable historical advice and criticism came from Dr. Max Myers, professor emeritus of economics at SDSU; and Professor Robert Thompson of the Northern State College History Department. The author's continuing advisor and thoughtful critic has been Dr. John E. Miller, professor of history at SDSU. Along with Dr. Miller, Dr. William Pratt of the University of Nebraska-Omaha and Dr. Louis Williams, professor of English at SDSU, and the author's husband, served as readers of the manuscript. The author acknowledges her debt to the three readers while assuming final responsibility for her manuscript.

Along with the materials in the Loriks papers, interview sources were crucial to the development of this manuscript. The major interview sources were Emil Loriks himself and his daughter, Ruth Ann Carlson, along with her husband, Vernon Carlson.

Others who were interviewed, either in person or by telephone, or who provided materials by letter, include the following: Halvor Stenson, Eleanor Johnson, Verna Lee, Marlene Duffy, Emma Turnquist, Pastor Conrad Krahling, Pastor John Haag, John Skage, the late Paul Opsahl, Ben Radcliffe, Ralph Sapp, Ervin Schumacher, Studs Terkel, Robert Handschin, Richard L. Johansen, John Barron, former Chief Justice Jon Fosheim, Homer Ayres, Martha Gustafson, Charlotte Gaard and Elin Swanson. Although not all of these individuals are cited directly in the text, all made contributions to the writing of this book.

Three of the author's former journalism students from SDSU—Chuck Raasch, Betty Burg and Tena Andersen Haraldson—all during the course of their newspaper careers have written about Emil Loriks and his work. We are especially indebted to Chuck Raasch for both his public tribute to Loriks at the time of his death and his comments in a letter to the author.

Finally, the author expresses her appreciation to her husband, Louis, and daughter, Katie, for their continuing support and understanding, and to her mother, Eleanor Evenson, for her support.

An Author's Preface

On the day after his death at age ninety on Christmas Day, 1985, Emil Loriks was eulogized by one-time *Argus Leader* reporter Chuck Raasch—"If anyone personified the spirit of South Dakota, it was Emil Loriks, a farmer and a gentle man who died Wednesday." By the time of Emil's death, it had been this writer's pleasure to have gotten to know this gentle man as well.

The friendship started on a May day in 1982, when the writer, then in search of a possible thesis topic for her M.A. in speech at South Dakota State University, happened to attend a noon luncheon meeting of the Brookings County Democrats at which Emil Loriks was featured speaker. He was at that time nearly eighty-seven. The sparsely-built Loriks, probably no more than five feet, six inches tall, got up after the meal and started to talk movingly, with not a single note in his hand, about the Great Depression of some fifty years before, and how he thought those events of the late 1920s and early 1930s bore striking similarities to the economic developments of the early Reagan Administration. In 1982 interest rates were reaching peak highs, as they had in the 1920s before the crash of 1929, and rural America was decidedly less prosperous than the country as a whole.

In twenty to thirty minutes, Emil Loriks had made the events of fifty years before come alive in his audience's mind, and he had, moreover, lover of politics that he was, gotten in a few good jabs at the administration of Ronald Reagan.

I knew after that speech I probably had my thesis topic—to write about some aspect of this man's public service and speaking career. This was quickly affirmed in a conversation with my thesis advisor at SDSU, and my next act was to write a letter to Emil Loriks at his home in Oldham, asking if I might come to see him, with a view to writing about him.

Before the first person-to-person meeting with Emil Loriks in the summer of 1982, I tried to find out more about this man who had started his public service career as a state senator in the 1920s and had gone on to be South Dakota Farmers Union president, a Congressional candidate against Karl Mundt,

Grain Terminal Association organizer, and ultimately its president for ten years, a state and later regional administrator for the Farm Security Administration, and national secretary-treasurer of the Farmers Union. I recalled having read his name in news stories over the years, and having also read some of his many letters to the editor.

Our first visit in Oldham in July 1982 confirmed that there was a real story to be told about the life of this gentle and unassuming man. Moreover, I found that he had boxes and boxes of personal papers and letters, then being stored at the Loriks-Peterson museum in Oldham. (Loriks had bought the former Peterson House in Oldham and given it to the local historical society to use for their museum—an act that demonstrates both his generosity and his desire to preserve historical information from the past.) In the fall of 1982, the papers were inventoried by a South Dakota State University professor under the auspices of the South Dakota Committee on the Humanities—this inventory proved an invaluable road map when I conducted my own careful perusal of the Loriks papers in the summers of 1984 and 1985.

The first stage in telling the story of Emil Loriks (and telling this story is something that has happened in stages; there was no grand plan to start with) was to gather some of the speeches Loriks gave during his forty plus years of public service. The South Dakota Farmers Union headquarters in Huron has back files of all *South Dakota Union Farmer* newspapers and in these worn and frayed papers are complete texts of all the radio addresses that Loriks had given over WNAX every other week during his term as South Dakota Farmers Union president in the mid-1930s. Also at Union headquarters are copies of state convention proceedings and in them the texts of the four presidential addresses that Emil Loriks gave. These Farmers Union speeches formed the bases for my selection of four speeches for rhetorical analysis. This thesis analysis had been preceded by a shorter study of some of Emil Loriks' persuasive practices as found in both his Farmers Union speeches and later reports he wrote and presented verbally as president of the Grain Terminal Association from 1957 to 1967.

My idea for a book about Emil Loriks was born gradually. The idea underwent additional development and nurturing during preparations for a series of two programs about Emil Loriks in October 1984, also done under the auspices of the South Dakota Committee on the Humanities. Humanities scholars and this writer attempted to put Emil Loriks' career into its broader social, historical and economic context, and Loriks himself was at the meetings in Brookings and Huron to help provide his perspective. With the help of further support from the Humanities Committee, the research of the Loriks papers, some fifteen boxes in all (which were by that time at the American State Bank for safer keeping than at the museum, which is not heated during South Dakota's cold winters), was completed. Throughout the research process, I turned to Emil for personal interviews, a tape recorder always at hand. His daughter, Ruth Ann Carlson of Minneapolis, was also part of some of these interviews—her participation still another indication of the graciousness the family showed in letting an outsider probe into their lives.

After Emil's death, I, of course, had many more questions on my mind, questions raised from the reading of the papers, which I had planned to ask him. I had last seen him on a sunny and brisk day in October when it was Emil Loriks Day in Oldham, and family and friends had gathered for a reception at the Oldham Lutheran Church to fete Emil and hear Governor Bill Janklow's proclamation honoring him. Throughout this fall, we had exchanged frequent letters, he from the Good Samaritan Center in DeSmet (where he had had to move in April 1985 because of somewhat uncertain health) and I in Brookings. His handwriting seemed a little less certain and some of his thoughts a little less sharp, but it was still a shock to get a phone call from Ruth Ann Carlson on Christmas Eve saying that her father was in the hospital in DeSmet with a buildup of fluids in his body and congestive heart failure. I quickly made plans to drive to DeSmet the day after Christmas to see him. The next noon, Christmas Day, Vernon Carlson, Emil's son-in-law, called to say that Emil had died early that morning.

Any hesitation that I might have had about finally getting started on the book about Emil Loriks died with him—I knew that this was something I must do. At this point, during 1986, I interviewed as many persons as I could (of those I had not already interviewed or written to during Emil's lifetime) and moved ahead with the writing of this book.

It is my hope to tell of this man's life, both its personal dimensions and considerable charm, but especially its major public service contributions. Emil Loriks was a major figure in South Dakota and Upper Midwest agricultural circles and in the public policy arena for some forty years. This will be a history of a man's public service career.

Chuck Raasch, in his eulogy of Emil Loriks, wrote, "As much as anyone, he lived the history of the state he so dearly loved. Here was a man with a story. As important as his story was, he'll perhaps be remembered more for how he told it: grandly, proudly, with spirit."

It is my hope to tell that story.

Elizabeth Evenson Williams
Brookings, South Dakota
September 15, 1987

Introduction

It is fair to ask why the story of the public service career of South Dakota agrarian Emil Loriks is a story worth telling. Loriks' career in the public service arena included service as a South Dakota state senator, as a Farm Holiday leader and organizer, as South Dakota Farmers Union president, as an unsuccessful Congressional candidate, as an administrator for the New Deal's Farm Security Administration, as secretary-treasurer of the national Farmers Union, and, finally, as president of the Farmers Union Grain Terminal Association, based in St. Paul, and the nation's largest grain marketing cooperative.

Just having held these positions, or at least some of them, would not necessarily mean that the subject should warrant book-length treatment. But there are several characteristics of Loriks' career that make his story unique.

As a young man fresh out of college, he trained to be a World War I pilot, although the war ended before he was called overseas. He came of political age during the New Deal, and the main thrust of his public service career was in the agricultural arena, especially his leadership as organizer of the short-lived and colorful Farm Holiday movement in South Dakota. Loriks' personality and approach, along with some other key factors, set the tone of the Holiday in South Dakota, making it a much more mainstream and even respectable entity than it was in other states, including neighboring Iowa and Minnesota. But at the same time, Loriks was an articulate spokesman, and, at times, even an agitator, for the concerns of the Holiday and depressed farmers in general and helped call needed attention to the plight of agricultural America during the depths of the Great Depression.

Loriks' life and career then must be examined as part of a New Deal and agrarian protest context.

Loriks' service as Holiday Leader and legislative leader (he served as co-chair of the legislature's joint appropriations committee in the 1933 session) put him on center stage of South Dakota politics. His service as state Farmers Union president from 1934-1938 was closely related to his work as a legislator in that he moved to have the Union formulate a positive legislation program, something that had not happened before. Moreover, Loriks and the Union were probably the reasons that South Dakota in 1935 enacted a gold severance tax against Homestake Mine of Lead, meaning that one of the state'e leading and wealthiest industries would have to do its share toward financing the affairs of South Dakota. Neither the legislature nor the governor wanted to act on the tax; the loud voice and impressive forces of the Farmers Union, however, as articulated by Loriks and enabled through the Union's statewide petition drive, meant that the taxation action was taken.

Loriks, whose public service career had begun with his election in 1926 as a Democrat to the state senate, moved to a larger state in the 1940s—beginning service in 1940 on the board of directors of the Grain Terminal Association, which he had helped to found, and also serving as national secretary-treasurer of the Farmers Union. Loriks was GTA vice president by the 1950s, and in 1957 began his ten-year tenure as the cooperative's president. This put Loriks into a prominent position, not only in his native South Dakota, but on the broader stage of the Upper Midwest, the GTA's service area, as well. His GTA position meant frequent trips to Washington, D.C., to lobby for legislation. While it is true that most of the real power of the GTA lay with general manager M.W. Thatcher, Loriks assumed important public relations and opinion-molding roles and was also skilled in enabling the strong personalities that comprised GTA management and its board to work together.

Even after his public service career was officially over, Loriks' was a voice that continued to speak out on farm and other public issues, and his counsel was still sought by those in positions of responsibility until the time of his death at age ninety in late 1985.

His is a story worth telling, and also a story that should be told as part of the ongoing history of agrarian politics in South Dakota and the Upper Midwest.

Emil Loriks, with his ever-present hat, in his early eighties.

Photo courtesy of Sioux Falls *Argus Leader*

CHAPTER I

The Early Years, 1895-1926

Emil Loriks was a son of the South Dakota prairie, born on his parents' Kingsbury County farm, between Arlington and Oldham, on July 18, 1895. Emil's father, Carl Gustav Loriks (the name was Lorikson back in Sweden), was the foreman of the Swedish immigrant railroad crew that laid the Chicago and Northwestern tracks across eastern South Dakota, as far west as Volga in 1879 and to Pierre in 1880. Carl Loriks and others of his fellow Swedish rail crew members decided to come back to Kingsbury County to homestead, Emil recalled, because there, "the grass grew tall and lush enough." This group of Swedish immigrants formed the basis of the Spring Lake Township settlement.

Within a fifteen-mile radius of Oldham, there were also Swiss, German and Norwegian settlements. In a paper about these early settlements in the Oldham area, Emil said that the seven settlements in the area "all seemed to follow a definite pattern of development. When established, their first priorities were to build a school, to educate their children, and to build a church for religious worship."

Emil's mother was Augusta Loriks, also from Sweden. Emil had an older sister, Emma, born in April 1894, fifteen months before Emil. He was christened "Carl Emil," but for the most part dropped the "Carl" in later years.

Kingsbury County is in the Prairie Plains area of eastern South Dakota and is characterized by grass which grows to a height of three feet and more. It is a semi-humid area, averaging from twenty to twenty-two inches of precipitation per year.

Late in his eighties, Emil recalled that he had spoken only Swedish at home until he started country school near his farm at age five. "I mastered English very quickly," Emil recalled, a mastery that was amply demonstrated by the countless speeches he gave in his long public service career. Emil began school at age five so that he could start the same year his sister did. There is just the suggestion that the young Emil would have been bored if he had had to stay home another year, and that his mother might not have known just how to keep him amused.

Emil went to his initial years of school in Kingsbury County, but when it came time to get more high school work than was offered there, he went to Huron where he stayed with an aunt and went to high school.

A young Emil Loriks (front left) is shown with his family, parents Augusta and Charles Loriks, and his sister Emma, probably shortly before 1900.

Photo courtesy of Ruth Ann Carlson

In 1910, when he was only fifteen, he traveled the twenty-plus miles from home south to Madison to take both pre-college and college work at Eastern Normal School, now Dakota State College. The hard-working Emil had to earn his own way through Eastern—relatives have recalled that his father gave him $10 and wished him well. Emil had a variety of jobs including working in the college president's office.

"I was ready for action when I got to college," Emil recalled. "Action" was what he got as he went out for a variety of extra activities, including debate, theater, the Webster Literary Society and being business manager of the college yearbook, the *Anemone*. He plunged into speech and other persuasive activities. He apparently had experience in declamation at either the high school or college level, and he took an "Oration and Argumentation" class at Eastern. He also took education courses, including practice teaching, that might well have helped to shape his persuasive efforts.

Both the 1915 and 1916 editions of the *Anemone*, the Eastern Normal yearbook, detailed Loriks' membership on the debating team. The debate group was called the "Strivers Debating Club," and in the 1914-1915 school year, Loriks was a member of the three-person team that debated the affirmative of the women's suffrage question, according to the 1915 yearbook. That yearbook describes the evening of April 11 at Oldham when the two teams from Eastern Normal presented their debate, and "the people of Oldham pronounced the discussion excellent in every respect and a credit to the Madison Normal." Perhaps this Oldham meeting was one of the debates for which Loriks recalled, "There was great public interest, many people came, and an admission [of perhaps 35 cents] was charged." (The audiences who attended these early debates perhaps provided him early training for speaking to the large audiences of 6,000 to 7,000 who attended the GTA meetings over which he presided.) Loriks emphatically recalled in the July 1982 interview that he refused to debate the negative side of the woman's suffrage issue! This statement would not only indicate that he held strong beliefs but might also have reflected a sense of identification with his fellow South Dakotans on the issue. As Herbert Schell reported in his *History of South Dakota*, South Dakota, in the 1918 general election, adopted a state woman's suffrage amendment to its constitution, ahead of the 1920 national action.

Whenever Loriks spoke of his debate activities, he was quick to speak of the influence of his coach Alice Lorraine Daly, described in the 1916 yearbook, as having "An M.A. from Emerson College of Oratory" and as a teacher of "Expression and Physical Culture." Loriks said many times that Miss Daly "inspired me," and his daughter also mentioned Miss Daly in the July 1982 interview as being a prime influence on her father's persuasive activities. According to the 1924-25 *Who's Who Among South Dakotans*, Miss Daly ran on the Nonpartisan League ticket for governor in 1922, having run on the same ticket for state superintendent of public instruction in 1920. This book also notes that she was the first woman to address a session of the South Dakota legislature. (It can be noted that Emil Loriks not only received Nonpartisan League influence from his father, but also from his debate coach at college. These influences may well have shaped his later thinking.)

Alice Lorraine Daly's name turns up later in the history of agrarian movements in South Dakota, and West River rancher Homer Ayres, with whom Emil Loriks exchanged many letters over the years, recalled that Miss Daly had been involved in somewhat "radical" causes with his father, Tom Ayres. The "beautiful Miss Alice" had been fired from her college teaching job because of her pacifist views.

Other extra-curricular activities at Madison also probably helped shape Loriks' later persuasive strategies. He was business manager of the *Anemone* for two years, and recalled during the July 1982 interview that he sold twenty pages of ads for one of the two years, "more than anybody had ever sold before." The 1916 *Anemone* noted his activities as business manager with a half-page display box which said:

> The members of the Junior Class wish to express their thanks for the faithful and efficient services rendered them by Emil Loriks. The success of the *Anemone* of both 1915 and 1916 has been largely due to his untiring efforts as business manager.

Loriks was also a member of the Webster Society, one of the three literary societies on campus. Each Monday during the chapel period, the three societies would present programs, and students "were rehearsed before presentation by the instructor in expression, who endeavors to aid the students in gaining good articulation, enunciation and expression," in the words of the 1915 *Anemone*. Loriks gained further experience in appearing before people by being a member of the junior class cast which presented the play "A Proposal Under Difficulties," in May 1916, according to the 1916 yearbook.

Loriks got a small taste of politics in college by being a junior class officer and a Strivers Debating Club officer, according to the 1915 yearbook. The 1915 yearbook described Loriks, in the caption under his picture, as "endowed with an intelligence above mere man." The 1916 yearbook said: "It was no broken reed you lean on when you trusted in his might."

Although Loriks wanted a degree in agriculture, he had chosen Eastern Normal because it did not have the mandatory ROTC requirement for male students that South Dakota Agricultural College at Brookings did. But after Emil had earned a first-class teaching certificate at Eastern Normal, but did not yet have the bachelor's degree, he decided to transfer to the University of Nebraska to get that B.S. in agriculture.

The recollections of the Nebraska years were not detailed in Emil's mind before his death, except that there was one year he spent in Alma, Nebraska, as a teacher and coach. The high school annual referring to this year's teaching experience is in the Heritage House museum in Oldham.

At any rate, after finishing his degree and teaching in Nebraska, Emil volunteered for service in World War I. His training took him south to Texas, where he trained as a biplane pilot. His nearly lifelong friend, Glenn Levitt, recalled that Emil had a reputation as a good pilot, one who was also a good mechanic and could fix anything. (Levitt explained in a 1986 interview that the reason the two men, both from Kingsbury County, probably never met before 1917 or 1918 when they did in Texas was that the Levitt family "traded" in Arlington while the Loriks family did their shopping in Oldham, which was closer to their farm than Arlington.)

Loriks completed his training as a pilot, flying stints in both Texas and Louisiana, but the war ended before either he or Levitt were summoned overseas.

After what must have been an exciting and even somewhat risky experience, given the primitive state of aviation at that time, Loriks came back to South Dakota and the family farm to work with his father.

Emil Loriks, in his early twenties, is shown in his World War I
Army uniform.

Photo courtesy of Ruth Ann Carlson

At some point after the war, Emil turned down a chance to
return to Eastern Normal as an instructor, choosing instead
the family farm.

The Loriks farm venture was a large one, horse-powered at
that time, of course. It was an extended family operation that
at one time covered twelve quarters of land and required
twenty-four horses. It was basically for corn, small grain and
hay. The farm home and buildings that were to be Emil's and

Ruth's after their marriage, and the place in which their daughter, Ruth Ann, grew up, were built across the road to the east of the original Loriks homestead. The "newer" Loriks buildings were unusual for South Dakota farm architecture in that they were brick.

There are still living in the 1980s older men in the Oldham area who as young men worked for the Loriks family as hired hands in those days of a more labor-intensive agriculture. Halvor Stenson, who once lived on the farm with the Loriks family, recalled the Loriks sense of humor, which Emil in later years perhaps tried to keep submerged to a certain degree. Stenson told a story about how Emil and he, who was ten years Emil's junior, had fun at the expense of a suitor of Emil's sister, Emma. One Saturday night, Emma's suitor had come for supper and she and the young man were visiting in the parlor after the meal. Halvor Stenson said that Emil took him aside to say that he planned for the two of them to go upstairs and then exit the house down a ladder Emil had leaned against the house. The two would then "have some fun with Alfred" by driving Alfred's Model T Ford to a hiding spot north of the trees. The two hid the car and then entered the house again up the ladder and came back downstairs to the parlor. Stenson recalled that Alfred quickly figured out what had happened and left the house in a moment of anger, and soon drove off in the car.

The Loriks family were leading members in the Evangelical Covenant Church, located just north of the Loriks farm. This was known as the "Swede" church in those days of ethnic churches, and had its roots in the Swedish Lutheran Church. The Covenant might be termed a "low church" Lutheran with its relative plainness of worship and lack of elaborate vestments. The Spring Lake Evangelical Covenant Church, which had been founded in 1891 due to a dispute with a Swedish Lutheran pastor who refused to bury a relative of one of the church families, held regular services until the 1970s, being serviced by a pastor who also served the church in Lake Norden. Even in 1986, the members of the church held an annual meeting, and the church opened for special occasions, such as that cold December day in 1985 when Emil Loriks' funeral service was held there and he was buried alongside his wife in the cemetery which is lined with the evergreens he had planted, and to which he had carried water.

Emil taught a few months in a country school northeast of
Oldham in 1921-22. The way the story was told by those who
remembered hearing about it, Emil was asked to take over a
rather unruly class in the middle of the year when the previous
teacher had failed to bring order. One of the things the
resourceful Emil did was to organize a basketball team to use
up surplus energy; he also developed the reputation of a hard-
working but fair taskmaster. Eleanor Johnson recalled that, in
the year during which Emil taught the country school, he let
her come back to the school, even though she had graduated
the year before, so that he could give her a couple of months'
instruction in Swedish.

Ruth Dahlen, by the time of these post-war years, was
becoming a factor in Emil's life. Her family, of Norwegian
background, had moved to the Oldham area from Mt. Horeb,
Wisconsin. Ruth had attended Eastern Normal, earning a
teaching certificate, and had come back to Oldham to work in
the post office with her father, who was postmaster. Later, she
was to become Oldham postmistress.

Few details of this courtship are available, although the two
were certainly aware of one another while both were in college.
The courtship was a lengthy one, and they were married on
January 12, 1924. Ruth Ann Carlson remembered that her
mother had said that the wedding "had to be at a slack time on
the farm." Ruth Ann was born more than six years later, on
November 30, 1930.

At some point during his early manhood, Emil Loriks
started taking an increasingly serious interest in politics and
in farm matters. Election records of Kingsbury County showed that in 1922, he made an unsuccessful try for Kingsbury
County superintendent of schools, polling 1279 votes to his opponent's 1361.

In 1924, he was one of five candidates in the November 4
general election running for state superintendent of public instruction. Running on the Farm-Labor ticket against a
Republican, a Democrat and two independents, he polled
24,413 votes to run third in the field of five. The Republican
C.G. St. John won decisively, polling nearly 92,000 votes or
more than twice as many as the second place Democrat.

In 1926, Emil made his first successful try for political office, this time as a Democrat running for the state senate in
usually Republican territory. He won over Republican Peter

The wedding picture of Emil Loriks and Ruth Marie Dahlen,
January 1924.

Photo courtesy of Ruth Ann Carlson

H. Schultz, by 1,594 votes to 1,209. In that same year, South Dakota voters re-elected their Progressive Republican Senator Peter Norbeck by an impressive margin, but ousted incumbent Republican Governor Gunderson and elected instead conservative Democrat William J. Bulow.

The then-Republican Sioux Falls *Argus Leader* called the 1926 election to the state senate of Democrat Loriks, "the election surprise of the year." Young Loriks, at age thirty-one, became the youngest member of the legislature. When Loriks entered the state senate, certain characteristics of his personality and public service commitment were firmly established. Many of these characteristics can be credited to the experiences of his early life. He had a solid family life, hard working to be sure. His father had had Nonpartisan League leanings. His favorite college teacher was a leader of radical causes.

Emil Loriks as a young man.

Photo courtesy of
Ruth Ann Carlson

Emil Loriks with his six-month-old daughter, Ruth Ann, in April 1931.

Photo courtesy of
Ruth Ann Carlson

Emil also had a strong sense of identification with farmers, who already by the mid-1920s were in the throes of an agricultural depression, although the rest of the nation did not officially start the Great Depression until October 1929. Years later, Emil said, "I sensed the lack of representation that farmers had, and I knew what their needs and their gripes were. Besides, I thought they were suffering from an inferiority complex."

This same sense of identification with those less fortunate was to be a characteristic of Loriks' entire public service career, and was in fact one of the Loriks qualities eulogized in the funeral sermon in December 1985.

Education seemed to be an important part of the Loriks background. It was probably a combination of his family's feeling it was important (although they did not give him a free ticket to college) and his own commitment. Loriks recalled in the early 1980s that he had grown up in a family that talked about things. At some point early in his life, he must have developed his interest in reading, for his later speeches are full of references to things he read. This love of reading continued to the end of his life, as this observer always noted books and magazines in great quantities, both at his apartment in Oldham, where she first visited with him, and also during the few months of his life at his room in the Good Samaritan Manor.

Emil had said that he was "ready for action" when he started college at Eastern Normal; he was no less so when he started his career in public life with the election of 1926.

CHAPTER II

Legislator and Farm Holiday Leader, 1927-1934

In 1926, Emil Loriks, who would mark his thirty-first birthday on July 18, had laid the groundwork for the public service career that was about to start. The public sector which Loriks entered in 1926 was a troubled one. Although the Great Depression for most Americans did not officially start until late in 1929, for South Dakota and other agrarian states, it started much sooner—not long after the boom years of World War I burst into a post-war agricultural depression. The conditions that were to lead to widespread agrarian protest, of which Emil Loriks was so noted a leader and spokesman, were developing in the 1920s.

The farm prosperity of World War I and immediately thereafter turned sour with a collapse of farm prices late in the spring of 1920, and by fall of that year conditions had "reached panic proportions," in the judgment of historian Arthur Link in *American Epoch.* By the spring of 1921, there was a "full-fledged farm depression."

The deteriorating farm situation of the 1920s was a complicated mix. There was decreasing overseas demand for American farm products, coupled with the enactment of high tariff legislation, which had the result of choking sources of foreign exchange in the United States and which made sales of agricultural surpluses abroad a virtual impossibility, according to agricultural historian John L. Shover. There was also widespread easy credit and "too eager speculation" during this period, Shover said.

At the same time, most of the rest of America was faring well. Link has described the 1920s as a time of increased productivity for American workers and of a rise in new industries like the automobile. But, as Link said, "The most important domestic problem in the 1920s was the agricultural depression that began in the summer and fall of 1920 and continued intermittently until 1935."

These adverse farm conditions stimulated the creation of the so-called "Farm Bloc" in the U.S. Congresses of the 1920s. The "Bloc" was an alliance of Midwesterners and Southern Democrats. The Farm Bloc took control of agricultural policy between 1921 and 1925 and pushed through Congress "the most advanced agricultural program in American history to that time."

In 1924, the McNary-Haugen plan was first introduced. McNary-Haugen was a two-price plan for American farm output. As historian Arthur Schlesinger, Jr., explained, there would be a protected price for the American market and a world price for the surplus thrown on the world market. There was to be an equalization fee assessed on owners of commodities to pay for the loss to the government.

McNary-Haugen had a tortured history, not being passed by both houses of Congress until 1927, and then being vetoed by President Calvin Coolidge. It was passed again in May 1928, only to be vetoed again. Although in the judgment of Schlesinger, the McNary-Haugen approach "would have been difficult to administer and worse of all, it had no means of stopping its higher prices from creating even greater surpluses," it was a reflection of the deep agony in the farm sector.

In the late 1920s, there were other suggestions for dealing with the agricultural depression, including voluntary domestic allotment, which was eventually to be incorporated into the first AAA of 1933. There was also the creation of the Federal Farm Board, but it, too, faced major problems because of shrinking foreign markets, dumping by other nations onto the world market, and its lack of authority to limit production or achieve domestic price stability.

In spite of the failure of McNary-Haugen, historian Link said of farmers that:

> By 1920, they had scored one of the most important victories in the history of American progressivism. They had succeeded not only in uniting farmers throughout the country into a solid front, but, more important, they had compelled the conservative majority in the Republican party to approve a federal farm program that included strict control of grain exchanges, stockyards, and packing houses, support for agricultural cooperatives, and credit facilities on

every level. From this advanced program, there would be no turning back; in fact, the pathway of progressivism point straight ahead to other advanced measures built upon the foundations laid during the 1920s.

It was this progressivism of which Emil Loriks was to be so much a part. "Black Tuesday," October 28, 1929, with the major collapse of prices on the stock market, marked the "official" start of the Great Depression for the nation as a whole. The Depression had multiple causes, including the unstable nature of the international economy, the long-standing depression in agriculture, and an unfair distribution of income that meant that 26 percent of the national income went to the top 5 percent of income receivers, even in 1920.

The stock market crash of 1929 was followed by an accelerating drop in already dismal farm prices. Wheat, which was $1.03 in 1929, dropped to $.67 in 1930, and to a low of $.38 in 1932. Hog prices fell from $11.36 per head in 1931 to $4.21 in 1933—the lowest prices since the 1890s.

Link has observed that the Great Depression has had a long-lasting impact, not only for "the havoc it wrought," but also "for the impetus it gave for completion of the metamorphosis in popular attitudes regarding the role of government in the economy."

As a predominantly agricultural state, South Dakota was, of course, part of the agricultural depression of the 1920s.

Historian Herbert S. Schell has explained in *History of South Dakota* that there was a sharp decline in farm income and a shrinkage of property values that made it difficult for farmers to fulfill obligations assumed during a period of high prices. There was a bank crisis in the making by 1925. There had been only one bank failure in 1921, but by 1925, 175 state banks had closed their doors in South Dakota.

Like the rest of the nation, South Dakota was governed by Republicans during most of the 1920s. But in South Dakota, the Republicans were of the Progressive persuasion, beginning with the Progressive Republican Peter Norbeck, elected governor in 1916, who served four years. (Norbeck was elected to the United States Senate in 1920 where he was to be an important part of the Farm Bloc and advocate of the later New Deal farm legislation, despite his Republican label.) Norbeck was followed as governor by another Progressive, William McMaster. There was a turn to conservative Republicanism in 1924 in South Dakota, with the election of Carl Gunderson, but in 1926, as already noted with the farm economy worsening in the state, conservative Democrat William J. Bulow ousted Gunderson and was elected governor. It was this same election that brought progressive Democrat Emil Loriks to the state senate.

Loriks served one term in the state senate but when he ran for re-election in 1928, he was defeated in a very close election, 2,407 votes to 2,341, by Republican J.C. Barber, a hardware and implement dealer from Hetland. In the November 4, 1930, election, Loriks challenged Barber for the senate seat, and won by 2,158 votes to 1,467 votes. Loriks won by an even bigger margin in his own Spring Lake precinct, 166 to 33. In the November 8, 1932, election that brought Democrats to power in both South Dakota and the entire nation, Loriks won easily over Republican John Bonde, 3,201 votes to 1,637, a two-to-one margin.

Even before coming to the legislature, Loriks had become involved in farm organizations. Robert Thompson, in his history of the South Dakota Farmers Union, reported that Loriks had joined the Producers Alliance in Kingsbury County shortly after World War I. This group was absorbed by the Farmers Union for a short time after the Farmers Alliance joined the Farmers Union, but he did not take an interest in it at the time. His interest for the next two or three years was with the Farm Bureau.

But, during his first years in the senate, he really came into contact with the Farmers Union. Thompson wrote that "he watched with interest the activities of President Batchellor and the Farmers Union and agreed with most of their legislative objectives. From this, he was led to believe that the Farmers Union had great possibilities for the future." Loriks joined the Farmers Union for a second time in 1930 and began to organize locals in Kingsbury County. In 1933 he was elected state vice president.

It was not until the early 1930s, 1932 in fact, that Emil Loriks was to emerge as an articulate voice of agrarian discontent and to be regarded as an agrarian leader. But the events of the early 1930s assuredly shaped Loriks' views on agrarian and political issues of a wider range.

Historian Schlesinger explained that while in 1919, farmers were receiving prices of 109 percent of parity (in terms of 1910-1914 prices), by 1929, the parity ratio was 89, and by 1931, it was a parity ratio of 64. Net farm income in 1932, Schlesinger said, was $1.8 billion, less than a third of what it had been three years before. Coupled with the sharp declines in farm prices was what Link called the "even more serious threat of foreclosure."

South Dakota economic conditions were "all but overwhelming," in the words of Herbert Schell, by the time the Tom Berry administration took office in early 1933. Between 1920 and 1930, real estate values had decreased 58 percent. The average value of farm land had fallen from $71.39 an acre in 1921, to $35.24 in 1930, and dropped to a low of $18.65 per acre within the next five years. The price of wheat on June 1, 1932, ranged from 50 to 55 cents per bushel, while oats and corn were selling at 22 and 29 cents respectively. Hogs brought $2.68 a hundredweight on the Sioux Falls market. The cash income from South Dakota crops decreased from $17 million in 1929 to $6 million in 1932, while income from livestock declined from more than $150 million to less than $45 million for the same year.

By the time Democrat Franklin Roosevelt was inaugurated President on March 4, 1933, there was widespread despair in the United States. Schlesinger wrote that the national income was less than half of what it had been only four years before. Some thirteen million Americans, or about one-fourth of the labor force, were out of work. The morning before the inauguration, "every bank in America had locked its doors."

Despite Roosevelt's hopeful words that "the only thing we have to fear is fear itself," there was to be continued suffering by American agriculture and by South Dakota.

As if the collapsing farm prices, threat of foreclosures and bank failures weren't enough, South Dakota and many other parts of the nation started experiencing severe drought. South Dakota writer-historian Robert Karolevitz has described the South Dakota despair of the 1930s:

> In July 1930 the temperatures soared above the 100 degree mark and persisted until crops shriveled in the fields. The intense heat began to take its toll of fat hogs and cattle, too, so farmers rushed them to market in a shipping flurry which forced prices

downward an additional notch. This was the beginning of the drought cycle which was to plague South
Dakota for the greater part of a wearying decade
which came to be known as the "Dirty Thirties."

In the 1932 election, the New Deal sweep, conservative
Democrat Tom Berry was elected governor and the Democrats
captured both houses of the South Dakota legislature. It was
this Democratic sweep that resulted in the elevation of Emil
Loriks to the co-chairmanship of the Joint Appropriations
Committee. Some of the Committee's and legislature's fiscal
actions in the 1933 session will be examined later.

Not surprisingly, given the deep depression that agriculture,
both in the Upper Great Plains and in South Dakota, was experiencing, there were significant political responses. The
significant vote polled by the Progressive party in the 1924
election can be seen as part of a general current of agrarian
unrest. The unrest spread to other sectors of society as the
Depression involved more and more people by the end of the
1920s and early 1930s. In 1932, the "Bonus Marchers," a
group of World War I veterans that wanted immediate payment of its pensions, came to Washington to protest, and after
Congress and the President had refused their demands, a riot
occurred when a police force attempted to clear a demonstra-
tion area. (Emil Loriks, in his later speeches of the 1930s, was
often to make reference to an uncaring President Hoover forcing the veterans out.)

The Upper Midwest, long the home of agricultural discontent, was again to be in the forefront of protest. Theodore
Saloutos has noted that the "western Middle West has behind
it a long history of agricultural discontent." Many major farm
organizations and movements like the Grange, the Populists,
the Farm Bloc, and the Progressives, as well as much of the
New Deal farm policy had their origins in the Middle West. It
is of more than passing interest to note that seven of the nine
secretaries of agriculture during the first four decades of this
century came from the western Middle West.

Perhaps the best known of the 1930s agricultural protest activities was the Farm Holiday movement—a movement in
which Emil Loriks was to play such a key role as executive
secretary-treasurer and organizer in South Dakota.

Interestingly enough, the Farm Holiday started at least in
part because of farmers' opposition to a test by state

veterinarians for TB in cattle. It was a bit later that the pro-testing farmers applied the principle of a bank holiday to agriculture—which led to the group's name. The farmers vowed to "take a holiday," and withhold the shipping of goods to market to effect a better price. By the spring of 1932, worsening agricultural conditions gave the idea of a farmers' strike new cogency.

To be sure, there was a basic dilemma inherent in the Holi-day's approach, a dilemma described by historian Arthur Schlesinger, Jr.:

> The Holiday movement made little economic sense. If mass withholding from the market might temporarily keep prices up, then release of the withheld produce would drive them down again. And only a minority of farmers in any case were prepared to take part in the movement. What the farm strike did was to throw into sharp relief the dilemma of a system incapable of using the plenty it produced, condemning millions to hunger because it lacked the wit or will to bring together the abundance and the need.

The founder and leader of the Farm Holiday was Milo Reno of Iowa, who served as president both of the Iowa Farmers Union and the national Farm Holiday Association. He was an aggressive advocate of "cost of production" as the basis for farm prices. Before being involved in the Holiday Movement, Reno had supported McNary-Haugen legislative efforts and had opposed the efforts of the Federal Farm Board. In its state convention in 1931, the Iowa Farmers Union had adopted a resolution favoring a farm strike. On July 4, 1932, the strike was called for in these words:

> Let's call a "Farmers Holiday"
> A Holiday let's hold
> We'll eat our wheat and ham and eggs
> And let them eat their gold.

Farm historians Theodore Saloutos and John Hicks de-scribed the early Holiday:

> By the fall of 1932, state units were in existence in Montana, South Dakota, North Dakota, Iowa, and other states. At no time was it [the Holiday] a

cohesive, well directed effort. From the start it appears to have been nothing more than a mob affair which first sought to keep farmers from marketing their products by peaceful means but next assumed the aspect of a group of angry, resentful men who want revenge against those of their kind who marketed their goods while they picketed and struck.

In South Dakota, as will be detailed later, the Farm Holiday was a much more restrained and even respectable movement that it was in other states like Iowa.

There was an angry Holiday incident in early 1932 in Sioux City, and then on March 12 and 13, 1933, less than ten days after Franklin Roosevelt became President, the Holiday assembled for a national convention in Des Moines. The Holiday gave the Administration date of May 3 to meet its cost of production ultimatum and other demands.

Also in early 1933, the Holiday shifted its emphasis from the farm strike formula in favor of efforts to stop farm foreclosure eviction sales and to enact farm foreclosure moratorium legislation. Perhaps the most violent anti-foreclosure incident occurred at LeMars, Iowa, just east of the South Dakota border, on April 27, 1933. Saloutos described what happened:

> Some six hundred people broke into a courtroom and demanded of the presiding judge that he sign an agreement not to execute any more foreclosure sales. When he refused, his assailants dragged him out of the courtroom. Upon continued refusal, he was blindfolded, taken to a crossroads, severely beaten and threatened with death. He did not sign the agreement. This outbreak placed the county under martial law. The assailants were arrested and sentenced, and no further serious outbreaks were reported.

Various states, including South Dakota, enacted legislation in response to the Farm Holiday's demands. Saloutos explained that in South Dakota, "a tax was enacted not on net, but on gross income; grace was extended in the payment of taxes; the general levy for 1934 was eliminated; and the assessed valuation of all properties was reduced by over $144 million."

The farm strike that the Holiday threatened for early May

1933 did not happen, because on the eve of the strike, Minnesota Farmer Labor governor Floyd B. Olson advised Milo Reno that "It would create more unfavorable sentiment toward relief than favorable." Holiday leaders called the strike off with the note that farm prices appeared to be rising, that farmers were too busy with spring planting and that there was a "sagging interest" among farmers. However, Holiday leaders did announce that they would closely watch the actions of the Roosevelt Administration.

The rapidly spreading Farm Holiday movement had surged into South Dakota in 1932. Robert Thompson explained that the leadership of the South Dakota Holiday was made up from and supported by five separate state groups. One member from each of these groups comprised the board of directors of the Holiday. The five organizations were the Farmers Union, the Farm Bureau, the Grange, the South Dakota Chamber of Commerce and the Bankers Association. Emil Loriks, who by this time was vice president of the South Dakota Farmers Union, was selected by the directors to be the executive secretary-treasurer, a post he held until in mid-1934 he became president of the South Dakota Farmers Union.

Thompson said, and South Dakota State University History Professor John E. Miller in his much later history of the South Dakota Farm Holiday agreed, that in South Dakota, the Farm Holiday was a much more conservative and restrained group than in other places. In later years, Loriks noted that in South Dakota, the Holiday was even asked by some merchants to come into their counties to organize as a way of directing and controlling farm discontent in an organized manner.

One of the reasons that Miller gives for the Holiday's subdued stance in South Dakota, as compared with that of neighboring states like Iowa, was in the character of its leadership, of which Emil Loriks was such a key part. Miller titled his history of the South Dakota Farm Holiday, "Restrained, Respectable Radicals," and cited four reasons for the Holiday's milder disposition in South Dakota—geographic influences, the historical development of farm protest activities in the state, political context, and the character of its leadership.

The South Dakota Holiday was most active in the more heavily populated areas of southeastern South Dakota, and except for Pennington County, there was little Holiday activity

West River.

The entire state, and not just the West River, has long had a reputation for being conservative, and the earlier Non-Partisan League in the late teens and early 1920s never was as strong in South Dakota as in Minnesota and North Dakota. To be sure, South Dakota had experienced its progressive impulses earlier with Coe I. Crawford, and in the late teens and early 1920s, with Progressive Republican governor and later Senator Peter Norbeck. It can be said that the Norbeck administration successfully co-opted much of the NPL platform.

While the emergence of the Farm Holiday in South Dakota in 1932-33 did reflect considerable agrarian discontent, the leadership of the state, especially in the administration of conservative Democrat Tom Berry, tried to deflect that agricultural protest by supporting the new farm programs of the New Deal.

There were, however, moments of emotion and excitement in the South Dakota Farm Holiday. In August 1932, conservative Republican Governor Warren Green was invited to address a Holiday board meeting in Huron. While indicating support for a planned withholding action in September, Green denied the possibility of peaceful picketing and repeated his intention to use his legal authority to keep the roads open.

Then the fiery John Simpson, the Oklahoman who was president of the National Farmers Union, rose to speak and electrified the crowd with these words: "If constitutions, laws and court decisions stand in the way of justice and human progress, it is time that they be scrapped." Nearly fifty years later, Loriks spoke of his disappointment with Warren Green, "All he could do was talk about law and order." Loriks also recalled that the crowd remained seated after Simpson spoke, not wishing to adjourn even though it had been told to, and that a mighty voice shouted back, "We want Simpson. We want Simpson. We want Simpson." So Simpson was brought back to speak again.

In his article, Miller discussed in detail the characteristics of the South Dakota Farm Holiday's leadership. Loriks and South Dakota Holiday president Barney McVeigh, who had been Republican Speaker of the House in the 1931 legislative session, insisted that farmers were not seeking "class legislation," although some of the Farmers Union literature of that day might tend to suggest otherwise. The fact that Loriks was a Democrat and McVeigh a Republican gave the South Dakota Holiday both a more moderate tone and a broader appeal, Miller said.

Loriks, who in 1932 and 1933 logged thousands of miles in his own car to organize local chapters of the Holiday (notes in the Loriks papers indicated that Emil Loriks filed for expresses of driving more than 10,000 miles from the formation of the Holiday in the state through July 1, 1933), was particularly active in the role of mediator between farmers with delinquent loans and the lending agencies that were seeking repayment. "Loriks' delicate position in the organization and his desire to retain certain credibility with both sides in disputes led him to avoid penny sales, but he was informed about them when they did occur," Miller indicated. Penny sales were relatively rare in South Dakota. (A September 5, 1933, letter to Emil Loriks from Farm Holiday worker Oscar Brekke of Albee, in northeastern South Dakota, tells Loriks about a tense sale at Milbank that netted $6.30, with a collection being taken up that netted just over $16, this being used to repay the pennies spent by the bidders and to buy lunch for guests from other counties who had come to the sale.)

Miller wrote that the "issues of picketing and violence constantly bedeviled the Farm Holiday leaders. Where they occurred, negative publicity and public resentment were the results, but picketing and roadblocks also seemed to bring results." Moreover, "spontaneous demonstrations by farmers revealed the depth of their discontent and prodded government leaders to respond." Emil Loriks was quoted in the Sioux Falls *Argus Leader* on September 22, 1932, as hoping that a peaceful strike would bring results, but "If prices don't go up, I suppose we'll have to resort to picketing." Miller observed that Loriks usually cautioned people against picketing and violence, emphasizing instead the need for cooperative and educational programs, but like others, "he remained ambivalent on the issue."

In describing the leadership of the South Dakota Farm Holiday, Miller noted that "cooperation with Main Street businessmen was a frequent theme of Emil Loriks, and the methods used by him and his colleagues in the Holiday movement to attract resources and support constitute the final explanation for the generally moderate tone" of the South Dakota Holiday. Although Loriks frequently cautioned against violent picketing, he also warned at times that picketing might have to be resorted to if peaceful protests were unavailing.

McVeigh, the Farm Holiday president, and Loriks, the executive secretary and organizer, were both members of the legislature—McVeigh having been House Speaker in 1931 and Loriks co-chairman of the Joint Appropriations Committee in the 1933 session—positions which "inclined them toward moderation and circumspection in their actions."

In a 1978 interview in the *South Dakota Union Farmer,* Loriks looked back on the Holiday which he had led forty-five years earlier and said that, while some of the Holiday's tactics would not have been considered legal, they were "the only expedient way to dramatize the farmers' plight so that the nation would be aware of the seriousness of the situation."

Some of Emil Loriks' rhetoric of the Holiday era, found both in his written columns as secretary-treasurer and in speeches that he gave, reflect both his careful style of leadership and also his willingness to call farmers to action. In a column written in October 1932, Loriks called the Holiday movement, "a crusade for economic justice for agriculture, the most widespread and far-reaching movement ever attempted, a crystallization of public opinion so tremendous that it cannot and will not be ignored." A few sentences later in the same report, he said, "The National Farm Holiday program is for orderly marketing of farm products and is interested in legislation to give agriculture a square deal. It does not contemplate nor does it countenance violence or disorder. It contemplates a campaign of education and persuasion, voluntary cooperation in withholding commodities from commercial markets for the cost of production."

In September 1932, speaking over radio station WNAX, Yankton, on the eve of September 21 "Holiday," Loriks rallied his farm troops with these strong words:

> We ask you farmers to STOP bankrupting yourselves and the business institutions of your towns by throwing your farm commodities on the market below the cost of production.
>
> Everybody realizes that cost of production for the farmers means prosperity for all.
>
> This is a call to service, a challenge to all good

American citizens! Volunteers! Minute Men! You
have a patriotic duty to perform. The eyes of the nation are upon us. Are we going to measure up to the
responsibility confronting us in this crisis, wherein
our homes, our country, and civilization itself is at
stake?

In the 1938 Congressional campaign, when Emil Loriks was
running for the First District Congressional seat against Karl
Mundt, and Farmers Union and Farm Holiday leader Oscar
Fosheim was running for governor, attempts would be made to
smear them as Communists. But Miller said that the records
suggest that these two men had steered their Holiday movement clear of the more radical United Farmers League, active
in the northeastern part of the state, and had avoided any kind
of cooperative action with the Communists such as occurred in
Nebraska.

There is a curious letter, May 15, 1933, in the Loriks papers
from H.M. Norfjor, editor of the *South Dakota News,* published at Wentworth. The letter begins, "Dear Comrade
Loriks," and speaks of class struggle and asks "YOU, have we
not?" even though others, such as John Simpson and Upton
Sinclair, were in agreement with the editor. As there is no copy
of an answer to this letter, it seems a safe bet that Loriks simply ignored it.

One of the continuing sources of internal tension for the
South Dakota Holiday movement was how to regard the
Roosevelt New Deal farm policy. The depressed agricultural
conditions had figured prominently in sweeping Republicans
out of office in 1932 in both Washington, D.C., and Pierre. During the last two months of 1932, Holiday spokesmen, both nationally and in the state, had a wait-and-see attitude toward
the new administration which would not take office until
March 4, 1933. Besides, South Dakota holiday leaders were
busy during South Dakota's January and February legislative
session dealing with the economic challenges facing South
Dakota.

Later in the spring, it did appear, at one point, as though the
new federal farm legislation might incorporate the Farm Holiday's cost of production into the bill. South Dakota did not
support the strike that national Farm Holiday leader Milo
Reno was planning to call in May 1933, and as already explained, Reno ended up calling off the strike at the last minute.

New Deal farm legislation was signed in May, but by fall, Agriculture Secretary Henry Wallace was quickly becoming a scapegoat for still disgruntled farmers. Farm Holiday leaders were accusing Wallace of having misled Roosevelt and they began calling for his removal. In a September 1, 1933 letter to South Dakota Farm Holiday leader E.N. Hammerquist, Milo Reno said:

> The present administration has had six months in which to work out a program for agriculture that would save the farmer from bankruptcy and ruin. Farmers everywhere are disgusted . . . .
>
> Secretary Wallace's base betrayal of the farmers who trusted him and the inhumanity of the program which he is responsible for has, in my opinion, destroyed any future possibility for service through him.

In a September 12 letter to Loriks, Reno said, "I believe that at the time of Mr. Wallace's appointment as Secretary, the majority of farmers were for him and had faith in his ability and integrity." He added, "There can be no relief for agriculture with Mr. Wallace occupying the new position of Secretary." Reno added that he did not think President Roosevelt was getting accurate information about farm sentiment, or else he would have replaced Henry Wallace.

In a Farm Holiday Association newsletter dated October 3, 1933, Emil Loriks warned his readers to prepare for a strike and added:

> Keen disappointment was expressed during the Special Session of Congress at Secretary Wallace's opposition to our Farmers Holiday program for *cost of production*, and more recently much dissatisfaction over his opposing inflation.

But the active days of the South Dakota Farm Holiday were nearly over. There were sporadic holding actions during October and November, Miller wrote. Monday, November 20, was designated "Justice for Agriculture Day," and all producers and buyers were asked to cease business for the day and all communities would be asked to protest "against the continued degradation of agriculture." "Justice for Agriculture Day" had mixed results—there was reduced marketing activity in some towns, but not in others, Miller explained. Governor Tom Berry went along with the Holiday and proclaimed officially "Justice for Agriculture Day" in the state.

With this occurrence, the major surge of Holiday activity in South Dakota was finished, although there were efforts to keep the movement alive in South Dakota in 1934 and even a couple of years after that. Perhaps the combination of New Deal farm policy and the movement of Emil Loriks from the Holiday leadership to the presidency of the Farmers Union in 1934, when then-state President Ed Everson assumed the national presidency on the death of John Simpson, resulted in the Holiday's demise in South Dakota. The last state farm Holiday convention in South Dakota was in 1934. Only in Iowa and Minnesota were there functioning state units of the Farm Holiday left after 1934, according to Shover. There were vestiges in many states through the mid-1930s.

Thompson said that the Holiday died because "Farm conditions by this time had started to improve . . . due to better crops and higher prices induced by the federal farm program. As conditions improved, there was less interest in and less agitation for such organizations." Historian Herbert Schell agreed, "The federal policies of farm relief under Franklin D. Roosevelt's New Deal Administration were diverting attention from the Farm Holiday program of direct action. Benefit payments were reaching the farmers by this time."

Amidst all this Farm Holiday activity and organizing, Emil Loriks was a member of the state senate and pursued various political concerns. In 1932, Loriks was offered the support of some Democratic party leaders to run for governor, but he turned the offer down, thinking that the odds against a South Dakota Democrat were too great, even in 1932, to justify mortgaging his farm to raise money for a campaign. The "draft" effort was corroborated by a campaign circular that Emil Loriks saved, and by an editorial from his hometown newspaper, the *Arlington Sun*, which referred to that campaign circular. The unsigned circular read in part, "Draft Emil Loriks for governor. Mr. Loriks is not only an honest-to-goodness farmer, but he is also a large owner of town and city property. Emil Loriks, who has never represented any faction."

It provides for interesting speculation to ask how Emil Loriks' life might have been different if he had agreed to run for governor. Might he not have won the Democratic primary and then the general election in what turned out to be a very Democratic year not only in South Dakota, but across the nation? One can also ask how his life might have taken a different path had he accepted the post-World War I offer of Eastern Normal to join its faculty? Would he have been like another Eastern Normal instructor, Karl Mundt, and later have entered politics, or would this have meant that South Dakota and Upper Midwest agricultural movements and organizations would not have had him as a leader and spokesman?

There was indeed a Democratic sweep in South Dakota in 1932. Not only did a conservative Democrat, Tom Berry, win the governorship over Warren Green by a 63.6 percent margin, but both houses of the legislature went Democratic as well. The Democrats were 29-15 in the state senate, compared with the previous Republican majority of 31-14, and the house went Democratic 68-34, compared with the previous Republican margin of 79-24. This meant that Democrats would control committee chairmanships and, as Loriks wrote in December 25, 1933 letters to Holiday figures C.M. Fonder and John Bosch, he had been asked by the Lieutenant Governor to be chairman of the Appropriations Committee. He added in the Fonder letter, "We are going to swing the axe, I hope," a signal of what would actually happen in the 1933 legislative session.

Governor Berry, who had campaigned on the need for government economy, proposed to the 1933 legislative session a budget of just over $8 million for the biennium, which was nearly $2.2 million below the budget for the previous biennium. The governor also proposed eliminating a number of departments, including the state sheriff's office, railway commission, state hail insurance, state bonding department, the securities commission, and other supposedly unnecessary parts of the state government.

But the legislature, under the guidance of such legislators as Loriks as chair of the Senate Appropriations Committee, moved to make even further cuts in the governor's budget. The final budget cleared by the legislature was $450,000 below the governor's proposed budget, with deep reductions coming in higher education and state employees' salaries. Nearly fifty years after all this had happened, Loriks was to express his regret that such deep cuts had to be made in education. Historian Thompson credits the South Dakota Farmers

Union, of which Emil Loriks was then vice president, as being "largely responsible for a reduction of $2.5 million in appropriations during the 1933 legislative session."

In some ways, it seems hard to picture Loriks as an enthusiastic state budget cutter, given his life-long support for educational and social programs. His willingness and even eagerness to lead the battle for budget cuts can be seen as a direct reflection of the difficult economic times and of the major drops in state revenue because of the farm conditions. Budget cutting was also a politically astute move.

There were other legislative concerns besides the deep budget cuts. There were concerns about taxation, with Berry's Administration favoring a gross income tax and farm groups wanting a net income tax instead. Despite the fact that 55 of the 103 members of the House were farmers, the farm group was unable to maintain a unified bloc in the legislature, and the gross income tax was passed over farmer objections. During the session, Loriks, the Farm Holiday executive secretary treasurer and Democratic Appropriations chairman, and Farm Holiday president Barney McVeigh, the GOP speaker of the House in the 1931 session, presided at meetings where they tried to unite legislators of Farm Bureau, Farmers Union, and Grange persuasion, but John Miller reported that the meetings did not succeed in establishing support for a single program. But he described them as a "moderating influence because of their tone of reasonableness and cooperativeness."

The issue for which Emil Loriks would later win the nickname of "Gold Dust Twin" (the other "twin" was fellow Farmers Union leader Oscar Fosheim), was a part of the 1933 session—the proposed gold tax to be levied against the Homestake Mine of Lead. An ore tax bill had been introduced as early as the 1927 session, and was a major subject of debate in the 1933 session, but did not pass. The careful Loriks and Farmers Union efforts in eventually getting a gold tax enacted in the 1935 session will be examined in a later chapter.

In his vice presidential speech to the state Farmers Union convention in the fall of 1933, Loriks reported:

> It was my privilege to take a leading part in the administration program as enunciated at Pierre. For instance, the gas tax, the Corey Gross Income tax, and I also sponsored your Farmers Union net income tax. My greatest opportunity for service to the

tax payers was as chairman of the Senate Appropriations Committee where with the many
Farmers Union members we succeeded in reducing
the appropriations to the tune of millions. The
greatest reduction that has ever been accomplished
in the history of the state.

In the same speech, Emil Loriks told the Farmers Union
that he had also represented their organization at the special
session of Congress "in the interests of your national
program."

Still another Loriks activity, as reported in the vice presidential speech, was to preside over a state tax conference, which
was instrumental in securing a further reduction in real estate
valuation of almost 12 percent, "which makes a total reduction
to date in the past three years of about 47 percent."

In those dark days at the end of 1933, in his vice presidential
speech, Loriks repeated his frequent theme that somehow
change would have to come without violence. "All history
records that all advancement has been made at the cost of
human life, but we believe if we become sufficiently organized
we should be able to do this without violence, bloodshed and
sacrifice of human life."

By the end of 1933, Emil Loriks, not yet forty years old,
had moved into a position of significant leadership, not only in
the Farm Holiday, but also in the state legislature.

CHAPTER III

South Dakota Farmers Union President and Agrarian Exponent, 1934-38

In March 1934, Emil Loriks suddenly found himself president of the South Dakota Farmers Union. Not quite thirty-nine, Loriks, as state Union vice president (to which position he had been elected the year before), became the president when the then-president of the South Dakota Union, E.G. Everson of St. Charles, who was also national vice president, moved into the top office upon the sudden death of President John Simpson. A March 18, 1934, letter from Alma Everson, Ed Everson's wife, to Emil's wife, Ruth, speaks at length about the trials both their husbands would face in their new positions. "I can sympathize with you knowing what you can expect since Emil is state president." Mrs. Everson wrote.

Within a short time, Loriks was to win re-nomination as a state senate candidate on the Democratic ticket and also a spot as a delegate to the Democratic state convention in the voting in the May 1 primary. However, as responsibilities piled up as the Farmers Union president, Loriks decided that he should do only that job, and so on August 27, he officially withdrew from the state senate race. In addition, he also resigned from his position as Farm Holiday executive secretary-treasurer.

Emil Loriks had been criticized in some Farmers Union circles for holding both the Farm Holiday and Union positions. There is in the Loriks papers a note in his handwriting:

> A communication just received condemns your State President for Farm Holiday connections.
>
> We plead guilty to being on the State FH Board together with the heads of all the other farm organizations—That is surely filling the place vacated by former President Everson.
>
> As state secretary, my resignation was tendered to the President and the Board at the time of the

state convention. Only part of the board being present, no action was taken and I was instructed to designate someone temporarily to do the work until the next board meeting.

Your State President's refusal to accept another term as secretary was emphatic and positive—and herewith is a copy of the resignation filed with the State FH president, June 7, 1934.

"Owing to the heavy duties developing upon me as the new president of the SD Farmers Union, demanding all my time and attention, I hereby tender my resignation as State Secretary.

—Emil Loriks"

Before examining Emil Loriks' career as South Dakota Farmers Union president, a post he held until mid-1938, it will first be appropriate to again consider the historical context of events. Economic conditions in both the nation and in South Dakota continued to be difficult, although not quite as bad as they had been during the time of the Farm Holiday's development in 1932 and 1933. There was severe drought in 1934, about which farm historian Theodore Saloutos has written. The drought, he said, "blanketed nearly three-fourths of the country and was described as being of unprecedented proportions in the history of the nation." By the late fall of 1934, in the Upper Great Plains, "the wheat crop was only half the average size, corn crop was the smallest in forty years, and the production of oats, rye and buckwheat was the smallest in more than half a century." The resultant smaller crops did lead to somewhat better farm prices.

In a WNAX radio address in 1934, state president Emil Loriks spoke of that drought. "Today, we face the most serious drought disaster in history! If it is crop reduction that is needed, we are getting it in a big way!" He said later in the speech, "Today, the big problem is to hold onto work and foundation stock and secure feed and water. Corn fields are withering and turning white, beyond all hope of recovery. Water supplies are drying up, cattle are bloating and dying on a diet of Russian thistles."

There were to be more weather problems in 1935 as well, with an outbreak of black stem rust in the spring wheat area in July, which reduced the prospective crop by more than 100 million bushels. The following year, 1936, was also a drought year, but the two following years did bring better growing conditions, but as a result, more farm surpluses and, thus, reduced farm prices.

In South Dakota in 1933, there had been a rate of seventy-eight farm foreclosures and bankruptcies for each 1,000 farms—a figure that was the second highest in the nation, behind only Iowa, according to data from John L. Shover. In 1934, the South Dakota rate was 64.2 such episodes per 1,000 farms.

South Dakota writer Robert Karolevitz in *Challenge: The South Dakota Story* noted that by the end of 1934, the number of South Dakotans on relief rolls reached 39 percent of the total population, the highest figure for any of the forty-eight states. In December 1934, more than one-half the farmers were on emergency relief. Historian Herbert Schell said that between 1920 and 1934, about 71 percent of South Dakota's banks had failed. He added that by the time the depression had run its course, the tax delinquency rate was ranging from 25 to 50 percent in a number of counties, a figure that certainly explains the impetus for the $2.5 million in state budget cuts made by the 1933 legislature.

It was against this backdrop that the new administration of Franklin D. Roosevelt moved to enact farm legislation.

The first Agricultural Adjustment Act was enacted in May 1933, too late to have much impact until 1934. Historian Arthur Link described it as "easily the most ambitious agricultural legislation in the history of the country." In its effort to attain parity, or the same relative purchasing power that farmers had held from 1909-1914, the AAA provided for imposition of various production controls. The money to finance the bill was to come from taxes levied on processing and from customs duties. A very controversial feature of the act was the plowing under of cotton and the slaughtering of pigs in 1933.

The Commodity Credit Corporation was established late in 1933 to provide crop loans for cotton and corn producers. Only a few weeks after taking office, President Roosevelt in late March of 1933 consolidated all the federal agricultural credit agencies into the Farm Credit Administration, which was followed by Congress' providing additional credit.

Link said that "the AAA worked an almost economic miracle until the Supreme Court called a halt in 1935." He added, "whatever the cause, farmers were well on their way toward stability and parity by the end of 1935." In South Dakota, historian Schell said that the provisions of the first AAA were "undoubtedly a factor in the price advance between 1933 and 1935; wheat, for instance, jumping from 30 cents to 90 cents a bushel, corn from 31 to 57 cents, and hogs from $3.50 to $8.35 a hundredweight." Other factors in South Dakota were the already mentioned 1934 drought and also a federal program which bought up surplus cattle from which the meat was canned and distributed to relief clients in the state.

Schell went on to say that the "government payments received by South Dakota farmers during the 1930s represented a substantial portion of their income." Furthermore, "AAA benefit payments virtually amounted to crop insurance for many who had suffered complete crop losses from drought and grasshopper infestations."

There were also other components of New Deal agricultural help. In 1936, the Soil Conservation and Domestic Allotment Act replaced the Agricultural Adjustment Act, which the Supreme Court had thrown out because of the processing tax. In 1938, there was a second AAA which retained the soil conservation features of the 1936 law and re-established the principle of acreage allotments as a means of adjusting crop production.

In June 1934, Congress, responding to radical farm demands, passed the Frazier-Lemke Farm Bankruptcy Act, which enabled farmers to recover lost property on easy terms. The Supreme Court unanimously overturned this legislation in 1935, but it was passed again by Congress, and in 1937 sustained by the high court.

Another major development came in 1937 with the passage of the Bankhead-Jones Farm Tenancy Act, called by historian Link "a landmark in the development of federal policy." The act sought to turn back the tide of increasing farm tenancy by reorganizing the New Deal Resettlement Administration into the Farm Security Administration, which had authority to lend money to enable enterprising tenants to become landowners, to refinance and rehabilitate farmers who were in danger of losing their lands, promise withdrawal of submarginal land, and to extend assistance to migratory workers.

In South Dakota, the Soil Conservation Act of 1936 meant

that some 90,000 farmers took part in soil conservation programs, for which they were paid a total of $15 million, according to Schell.

From May 1933 to July 1938, just over a five-year span, the Farm Credit Administration loaned a total of $83.4 million to South Dakota farmers. The New Deal also included relief measures, and South Dakota, through a tax on beer passed in 1933, also provided relief.

Not unexpectedly, there were a number of political responses to the agricultural depression. The Farm Holiday, already discussed, was a major reaction to distressed farm conditions of the early period of the Depression. The entire legislative program that Emil Loriks and the South Dakota Farmers Union supported, at national and state levels, was also a significant response to depression conditions.

Before noting Farmers Union ideology and actions and the role that Emil Loriks played as state Farmers Union president, it is important to note, at least in passing, the revolt against both the depression conditions and the New Deal handling of those conditions embodied by Father Charles Coughlin and Louisiana Governor (later U.S. Senator) Huey P. Long, Jr. Both Fr. Coughlin and Long were originally New Deal supporters, but later came to vigorously oppose New Deal measures. Radio priest Father Coughlin became involved with agrarian protest by 1936 when he actively backed the Frazier-Lemke farm mortgage financing bill. Coughlin went on to organize Congressman Lemke's unsuccessful Union Party presidential bid.

At least part of the Farmers Union became involved in that third party movement in 1936, when E.E. Kennedy, who had been national Farmers Union secretary and editor of the national newspaper until he was voted out of office at the 1936 national Union convention, backed Lemke. Kennedy's actions on behalf of Lemke produced a split in Union ranks, according to Shover.

Long has been widely regarded as a demagogue in the years since his power in Louisiana and national politics, although not all historians share that view. Link described him as a "dangerous menace to American democracy," while historian T. Harry Williams, in his sympathetic biography of Long, *Huey Long,* pointed to many accomplishments such as educational improvement and road building during Long's term as

Louisiana governor, and saw in Long a "mass leader," who appeared at a time when his state was ripe for reform and a mass movement.

As early as 1933, Long turned away from his earlier support of the New Deal and was widely believed by the time of his assassination in 1935 to be planning to challenge Franklin Roosevelt for control of the Democratic party and to run as president, either as a Democrat, or at the head of a third party.

Some of Emil Loriks' most interesting rhetoric during his tenure as South Dakota Farmers Union president dealt with Coughlin and Huey Long. In addition, early in the New Deal, Loriks and the Farmers Union tended to be critics of the New Deal for not doing enough to help farmers, although the comments varied from time to time. The Union after 1936, when its leadership changed, became a New Deal supporter.

Before examining Emil Loriks' tenure as state Farmers Union president, it is necessary to describe briefly the politics and ideology of the Farmers Union, and to look briefly at its history.

The Farmers Union was founded in Texas in 1902 by newspaperman Isaac Newton (Newt) Gresham. Gresham had earlier been active in the Farmers Alliance and in the Populist movement. In 1905, the Farmers Union became a national organization. The Union came into South Dakota in 1914. During the World War I years, the national Farmers Union organized cooperatives, which were to become strong, particularly in the north-central states by the 1920s. William Tucker, who has studied the Union, said that the cooperatives included purchasing as well as terminal grain and livestock marketing. The Farmers Union backed the ill-fated McNary-Haugen bills of the 1920s, and was part of the Corn Belt Committee, a federation of many farm interests that lobbied for farm legislation from 1925 to 1930.

Tucker, in a 1947 article in *Agricultural History* on the Farmers Union, also credited it for being responsible for "one of the most picturesque 'farm revolts' in American history—the Farm Holiday movement."

Historians are not in firm agreement about the Union's stance toward New Deal legislation, even though, as will be seen in the discussion of the South Dakota Union, Loriks sharply criticized certain aspects of early New Deal farm policy, and was especially scathing in his comments about

Agriculture Secretary Henry A. Wallace. Tucker wrote that "the Agricultural Adjustment Administration and subsequent New Deal agricultural legislation met a mixed reception from Farmers Union leaders." He, however, did indicate that the spring wheat area, of which South Dakota is a part, "supported the Agricultural Adjustment Administration and prepared the first commodity program under it, namely the one for wheat, including a crop insurance feature." Later in the New Deal, the Farmers Union became a much stronger New Deal supporter, which is reflected in Loriks' rhetoric and political actions toward the end of his term as Farmers Union president.

John Crampton, in his *The National Farmers Union: Ideology of a Pressure Group*, wrote, "It did not favor with enthusiasm the New Deal farm programs it later came to support wholeheartedly. . . . However, its remedies were more, not less, radical than the New Deal programs. In most non-farm issues (such as the enlargement of the Supreme Court), the Union did support the New Deal."

A major thrust of the Farmers Union, which continues to this day, although under a different name, was its grain-marketing efforts embodied in the Farmers Union Grain Terminal Association (GTA)—now known as Harvest States. It became the nation's largest grain marketing cooperative. Loriks was one of the state Farmers Union presidents who helped to set up the GTA in the late 1930s and served on its board of directors for twenty-seven years, the last ten as president, from 1957 to 1967.

Robert Thompson, in his history of the South Dakota Farmers Union, said that the years of the agricultural depression, from the 1920s through the mid-1930s, found the power of the Farmers Union shifting from the south to the northern plains and the interests of the group shifting more to legislative and political action.

Students of the Farmers Union have noted what they term a "split personality" of the group, in that one segment has always put more weight on the cooperative marketing approach as a way of working through the agricultural dilemma, while the other group has tended to want to involve the federal government to stabilize farm prices and to protect cooperatives. In a sense, Loriks' actions can be seen as an illustration of that "split personality," in that he was both an active politician and also a significant cooperative exponent in his long career.

Tucker described the Farmers Union in these terms: "Throughout its history, the Farmers Union has been the general farm organization most closely identified with militant agrarian reform since the days of the Farmers Alliance." He continued, "As one aspect of continuing the Populist tradition, monopolies and middlemen have been consistently opposed, while the maintenance of the family-type farming system has been a basic objective."

The Union, perhaps, was not (and may still not be) as militant as it may have appeared. Saloutos said:

> The Union was by no means the radical organization that its language made it out to be. It sought, with a limited degree of success, to teach farmers that they could live within the capitalistic system. The emotional and strongly-phrased language employed in condemning the existing order was but a means used by the Union for selling itself to depressed farmers who did not respond to other appeals. This enabled it to enroll members in areas where other groups had failed.

Crampton, in his study of Farmers Union ideology, described the organization's style as being "marked by belligerence and by optimism. The Union's casual rhetoric bristles with the language of struggle. The organization calls itself, 'militant, aggressive, hard-hitting, ongoing, vigorous, outspoken, the vanguard.' " He added, "The Farmers Union is a protest organization; it seeks a gadfly role," and noted that the Union has always drawn heavily upon the prevailing tone of each generation's liberalism. "It has always been ready to adopt as its own the current progressive reform and dissent." Crampton isolated four strands in the Union's ideology—the sense of disadvantage, pacifism, cooperativism, and the family farm ideal.

The South Dakota Farmers Union carried the same ambivalences characteristic of the national organization. Thompson said that many South Dakota Union leaders favored a combination of emphasis on both cooperatives and on a political legislative program. Emil Loriks, in fact, did. Thompson said that "the faction that favored cooperatives had the complete support of President Loriks [1934-1938], and it is probably correct to say that it was during his administration that the cooperative groups were recognized by the leadership of the Farmers Union program in South Dakota." However, Thompson went on to say that Loriks was the state Farmers Union president responsible for introducing a change of tactics in dealing with the state legislature—"the introduction of a vigorous legislative program." "Loriks began to work for more harmony by supporting desirable legislation and actually formulating a legislative program." Loriks' presidential style can be attributed to his own legislative experience and the contacts that he had with various legislators, as well as to the fact that a number of Farmers Union members were also members of the legislature in the 1930s.

An idea of the Union's political stance of the later 1930s can be found in a statement developed at a meeting of Farmers Union representatives with other progressive organizations. Among the items in their program were federal aid for South Dakota, higher taxes for higher income brackets, a tax on state corporations doing business in the state, a tax on large gifts, inheritance and undivided corporate profits; increases in the ore tax; opposition to further sales taxes, ratification of the child labor amendment; support for civil liberties, adequate aid for public schools; and support of a non-partisan primary law.

The membership figures during Emil Loriks' presidency followed the ups and downs of the farm economy. While the South Dakota Farmers Union lost 3,034 members from 1931 to 1933, "reflecting the adverse economic conditions existing in South Dakota during these years," in 1934 and 1935, there were gains of 1,486 and 617, for a total of 6,763 members in 1935. Thompson credited those gains to the impact of the Farm Holiday Association. In 1936 and 1937, there were losses of 1,152 and 1,149, respectively, while in 1938, numbers leveled off, with a small gain of 32, for a total of 4,430. These losses "once more reflected the economic plight of the farmers. Part of the decline is attributable to the drifting away of many of the new members who had joined in 1934 and 1935, but who soon lost interest in the organization," Thompson said.

In addition to his "constructive program of farm legislation," Thompson also credited Loriks with developing a "more mature viewpoint" in Union dealings with the rival organization, the Farm Bureau. The Farm Bureau, by state law, was part of the agricultural extension program, and the Union had opposed the Bureau and had hoped to destroy the State College Extension program and the county agent program, "all for the purpose of ending the favorable advantage to the Farm Bureau. But its attempts to damage the Bureau failed and only intensified the bitterness."

Thompson continued:

> Emil Loriks handled the Farm Bureau problem in a more positive and constructive manner. Instead of continuing the fight to destroy the extension and county agent program, Loriks solved the Union's problem through an effort to separate the Farm Bureau from the State College extension program. This was accomplished by legislation in 1935. This legislation removed much of the friction that had existed between the Farm Bureau and the Farmers Union prior to 1935.

Perhaps because Emil Loriks had at one time briefly been a Farm Bureau member, it made it possible for him to help remove the bitterness between the two organizations in South Dakota.

An editorial from the *South Dakota Union Farmer*, the organization's newspaper, written in the 1940s at the time Emil Loriks was elected national secretary-treasurer, praised him for his accomplishments as state president:

> During the many years Loriks was state president of the South Dakota Farmers Union, he never chose the easy, negative road of blind denunciation and fault-finding. He did not waste his time merely talking about out problems. Loriks is a postive personality, a builder, a man of action. He led the fight against the powerful Hearst interest, resulting in an ore tax of over a million dollars a year for the state of South Dakota collected from the Homestake gold mine. Other legislative victories followed, resulting in lower taxes and lower interest rates, all designed for the benefit of the family type farmer.
>
> Acting in harmony with his convictions, he launched a most ambitious program of building cooperative oil companies during 1934, 1935 and

1936, just at the time our people were hardest hit by drought, grasshoppers, and hard times.

Thompson wrote this about the South Dakota Farmers Union:

> Since its organization in South Dakota, the Farmers Union has remained an important farmers' organization. This will continue as long as the Farmers Union remains an important farm organization and practices its philosophy with the same vigor it has exhibited in the past.

The crowning achievement of the South Dakota Farmers Union during Emil Loriks' tenure as president, if not for its whole history, was its successful effort to get the legislature to enact the gold severance tax. This was finally accomplished in the 1935 legislative session, but the story was neither short nor easy.

The gold tax had first been introduced in the 1927 legislative session, and major efforts were also made in the 1933 session. Because of national government actions in 1934, the idea of taxing the Homestake gold mine in South Dakota gained even greater impetus. The Federal Gold Reserve Act of 1934 established the price of gold at $35 per troy ounce, meaning that the production of Homestake would be purchased by the government at a guaranteed price.

This guarantee of prosperity to Homestake came at the very time when the rest of the state "was struggling through the Bleak period," in Karolevitz's words. "An air of prosperity prevailed as the work force was expanded at Homestake." In 1934, Homestake sold $16.5 million worth of gold, and Homestake stock shares reached $430, compared with the pre-Depression price of $50.

Thompson has written of the Farmers Union role:

> Perhaps the Farmers Union had outside assistance in the enactment of the ore tax legislation. The fact remains, however, that the organization was very active in carrying this issue to the people and developed the strength necessary to enact the ore tax bill. It should also be noted that during the 1930s, a larger proportion of the legislature was affiliated with the Farmers Union than at any other time.

The Union strategy for the eventual passage of the ore tax was astute. After the tax failed in the 1933 legislative session, the Farmers Union in 1934 spearheaded a huge petition drive for an initiative to put the ore tax on the ballot, should the 1935 legislature fail to enact the tax. Union leaders, however, held the petitions as a bargaining chip as the 1935 session started.

The Farmers Union rationale for this tax was presented in a statement made by State Senator Emil Loriks before he assumed the Union presidency.

> Shall we tax distressed farmers, laborers and merchants more, or shall we look to an untapped source of revenue in South Dakota?
>
> Practically every state in the Union, rich in mineral resources, has ore taxes or severance taxes. South Dakota seems to be the exception!
>
> We have in South Dakota, what is reputed to be the richest gold mine in the world, exploiting our natural resources without paying a just compensation to the state for that privilege. According to a S.D. highway booster map, we have here in the Black Hills, "the richest hundred miles square on the earth."
>
> From 1875 to 1932, our gold resources in South Dakota were depleted to the extent of $308 million, according to the U.S. Bureau of Mines without ever paying one thin dime of tax on production.
>
> In this year 1934, Homestake will gross approximately $18 million due to the increased price of gold from $20.67 per ounce to $35. This increase is equivalent to a bonus of about $8 million in addition to their already swollen profits.

Loriks went on in this statement to say that "while the power to legislate is vested with the legislature, the people expressly reserve to themselves the constitutional right to propose measure as a last resort—or as an alternative to legislative inaction." Loriks added that the initiative petitions would be filed with the Secretary of the State if the 1935 session failed to act.

Union President Loriks charged Farmers Union members, as they carried their ore tax petitions, to "put those who aspire to serve you in the legislature on the spot. If they are not for the ore tax, *leave them home!*" In the same newsletter, Loriks said that the "state Union car is now equipped with loud speaking systems, and in the course of a Wednesday or Saturday evening, we often address three or four good audiences."

The ore tax battle was not without its moments of levity. In one of Emil Loriks' scrapbooks were found lyrics called, "Why Tax Gold," to be sung to the tune of "Beulahland." The words for this song, one of many sung by Farmers Union members at their meetings, were as follows:

by Ethel Feenefos, Midland, S.D.

WHY TAX GOLD

1. They've taxed your wheat
     They've taxed your bread
   They've taxed your stock
     And the things they're fed
   They've taxed your land
     Your gasoline
   And have left you farmers
     Slick and clean

CHORUS
Oh, Dakota Land,
  South Dakota Land
Here on thy barren soil stand
  From North to South
From East to West
  There's not much left
For man or beast
  They have your cattle
Hogs and wheat
And left you people on relief

2. You've been the ball,
     You've been the bat
   You've stood for this
     And stood for that
   The game is won
     With tools they're done
   But now your game has just begun.

CHORUS

3. It must be riches now that's taxed
   To raise the burden from your backs
   They have the means with which to pay
   So pass the Ore Bill without delay

CHORUS

4. This tax is fair in every way
   For those with profits have to pay
   The little miner with income small
   Don't have to pay this tax at all.

CHORUS

5. We've had the Gross Sales Income Tax
   But there's not much revenue in thistles tax
   With drought and hoppers year on year
   We must tax gold now it does appear

CHORUS

6. You men in office heed the call
   Save South Dakota from her fall
   Tax that which really belongs right here
   And show your courage instead of fear

CHORUS

7. She has this God given wealth in store
   On which she's never drawn before
   The time has come
   She must use it now
   To keep her great name in renown.

CHORUS

The above contribution comes from Western S. Dakota

When the 1935 legislative session started in early January, Emil Loriks and his Farmers Union troops were ready. Loriks spent the session in Pierre, with Union Headquarters at the Waverly Hotel, and kept his membership informed through frequent newsletters, newsletters which form the basis of the ore tax story told here.

At the start of the session, Loriks wrote, "We're off to a good start. Both sides are girding for the fray, the *battle of the century*. It will be a titanic struggle between the forces that have dominated the state for the last half century on one hand and the people on the other."

He continued, "The ore tax is the burning issue. While the matter of additional revenue is important, the real issue is *who is going to determine the policies of government in South Dakota*, the people or the privileged few. The ore tax will be the acid test, whether legislators or public officials are for or against the people."

In addition, referring to the reduction of state appropriations by nearly $2.5 million in the 1933 session, Loriks said, "the present session is going to tap a new source of revenue that is going to help maintain our government, its institutions, its credit and perhaps help to alleviate suffering and distress. This is going to be a historic session."

By early February the campaign intensified. A rally was called for February 10 in Sioux Falls to discuss the ore tax. Loriks also took to WNAX to answer ore tax opponents, after "criminal lawyer Tom Kirby" had gone on a two-station hookup to oppose the tax. Loriks pronounced himself gratified with the favorable response after the Farmers Union radio reply to Kirby. In the February 6 newsletter, Loriks urged his readers to write their legislators immediately. "Encourage them in this fight, for they are up against the heaviest artillery ever faced by any legislators in South Dakota history. Sorry, we cannot enclose checks as the opposition is able to do, but, people, this is your fight."

On February 22, Loriks reported the successful efforts to amend the Senate bill into a tax form unacceptable to the Farmers Union, after an acceptable bill had passed the House. He called the Senate bill, "a fake substitute." The Senate bill had the support of the Democratic administration of Governor Tom Berry.

At this point, State Union President Loriks announced that the petitions circulated by the Union in 1934 would be filed, thus forcing the ore tax issue to a vote of the people. "This will make it mandatory for the legislature to submit the ore tax to a vote of the people," Loriks was quoted as saying in the *Evening Huronite*. There were some 22,000 names on those petitions. The Farmers Union newsletters also carried records of the roll call votes in the legislature to date on the ore tax.

The House, in its second vote on the tax, refused to adopt the Senate's ore tax substitute measure, or "illegitimate ore

tax baby," as Loriks called it. So the two bills went to conference committee to be reconciled.

The conference committee, after eighteen hours of delibera-
tion, struck a compromise which the Farmers Union would accept. Instead of a 10 percent tax, the revised bill called for a
gross income tax of 4 percent on the mining industry, with a
deduction to protect smaller mining operations and safeguard
new development. In reporting to Union members on February
28, Loriks wrote that the tax would probably yield about
$700,000 to state coffers in 1935.

Loriks explained the rationale for accepting a compromise.
For one thing, it would mean immediate revenues to the state,
rather than waiting until after the issue could be voted on by
the people in the 1936 general elections, as the initiative route
would dictate. Some $2 million would have come into the state
treasury by the time this initiated law could have been passed
and put into operation.

Loriks called the day the new compromised was passed a
"red letter day" in South Dakota as well as in Farmers
Union history. "This fight is won. The Farmers Union has
established once and for all the principle of an ore tax in
South Dakota."

In the same newsletter in which he reported on Farmers
Union success, Emil Loriks could not resist replying to
those of the state's press who had asserted that the
Farmers Union had too much power in the legislature. The
editor of the *Redfield Press* had accused the Farmers
Union ore tax bill of being "written by men unfamiliar
with the mining industry, their leaders are unwilling to
give an inch and prefer no tax to a just one" (referring to
the senate substitute bill). The editorial had continued by
saying, "For a number of years, the Farmers Union has
had the desire to control the legislature in this state. At
last, their desire has been accomplished and they are in
full power." To which Emil Loriks wrote, "Thus you can
see how the reactionary press fears the Farmers Union."

To be sure, during this time when the Union was urging
"Tax Gold, Not Poverty" in its posters, the Homestake Mine
was vigorously opposing ore tax proponents. In its many ads,
the mine pointed to the numbers of persons it employed, and to
other state and federal taxes it had paid. A Homestake ad indicated that the 1934 tax figure amounted to $105 tax per ton,

including both state and federal taxes.

In the same ad, Homestake said it had produced $253 million in gold, a figure less than the $300 million plus cited by Emil Loriks.

Loriks understandably savored the Farmers Union ore tax victory. In his 1935 presidential address to the state Farmers Union Convention in Yankton in October, he said:

> Against us were arrayed powerful political groups, powerful corporation interests, and a horde of corporation attorneys and professional lobbyists. We were confronted with opposition from the most powerful financial interests in the state. The opposition was identified with powerful interests that reach from the Atlantic to the Pacific, interests identified with perhaps the most far-flung newspaper in the world (Hearst), interests that have controlled the state of South Dakota for half a century.
>
> Do you wonder that the Farmers Union had a big fight on its hands? It was like David going up against Goliath.
>
> The ore tax may not be all that we wanted, but it is a mighty big step in the direction of taxing wealth, taxing those most able to pay. We have established the principle. We have set up the machinery. We have tapped a source of wealth heretofore almost untouched.

In addition to pointing to the ore tax success in the 1935 legislative session, President Loriks was also pleased with other political developments. One, in his words, was that "we have established the principle of a net income tax for the first time in South Dakota." In the 1935 presidential convention speech, Loriks said that he hoped that the ore tax and the net income tax would eventually produce enough revenue so that the sales tax could be dropped. In 1935, the Farmers Union, together with the South Dakota Railroad Commission, was successful in getting a decrease in freight rates, something that would help South Dakota farmers.

Fifty years later, in talking about the ore tax battle, which remained one of his favorite topics of conversation, Loriks recalled that at one of his speeches in the West River area, he was confronted by a group of Homestake miners, who claimed they would lose their jobs if the tax were enacted, and who in Loriks' words, "threatened to hang him from the nearest tree." He continued, "I really felt sorry for them."

As important as the discussion of the ore tax bill is in examining Emil Loriks' tenure as Farmers Union president in South Dakota, it is also necessary to consider his handling of the internal politics of that organization, for it did not always speak with one voice.

Just a month after assuming the Union presidency, Loriks noted in a letter how busy he was. "Am fortunate indeed if I find an evening at home, for I am on the road about all the time, making meetings in nearly every county of the state." At about the same time, in a letter to Congressman Fred Hildebrandt, Loriks said that "this Farmers Union presidency will take all my time."

In a letter to fellow Union members, Loriks wrote on April 3, 1934:

> Personally, I have gotten to the point where I pay little attention to all the barking and snapping at my heels. I keep my powder dry and conserve my ammunition for the opportune time. For instance, one disgruntled politician, editorial writer in our county seat paper, has been sniping at me ever since the last election. I have not even recognized him by an answer, but when the psychological time comes, I am going to take him to a cleaning that he will never forget.

During his term as SDFU president, Emil Loriks always had a strong sense of identification with his members. He wrote to Oscar Fosheim late in 1937, "Just traded my V-8 for a new Chevrolet, so I am in line with the rest of you fellows traveling the highways."

From time to time, there was apparently speculation about Emil Loriks' political plans. A letter from a doctor in Alexandria, in February 1934, just weeks before Loriks became Farmers Union president, suggested that Loriks accept the nomination for lieutenant governor. He replied to the doctor after becoming president, "Personally, I am not aspiring to any high political office just now."

The struggles within the South Dakota Farmers Union,

which culminated with Emil Loriks' resounding re-election as state president in October 1937, were set in the context of the struggle within the national organization. Crampton, in his book about the Farmers Union, explained that the struggle of the 1930s was primarily one of ideology, between radical and more moderate factions. The dissent had actually started in the 1920s over the National Union leadership's decision to support the Federal Farm Board under the Hoover Administration.

In the national organization, the so-called "radical" faction dominated from 1930 to 1937, and certainly included the presidencies of John Simpson (1930-1934) and Ed Everson (1934-1937). The more radical faction strongly opposed most New Deal farm policies. Other leaders of the radical faction were Milo Reno, already discussed in his role as Farm Holiday leader, and E.E. Kennedy, national secretary of the Union from 1931 to 1936 and a follower of Father Coughlin. The moderate faction was more friendly to the New Deal, and one of its spokesmen was M.W. Thatcher of Minnesota, of the Northwest Organizing Committee. (Loriks' life and Thatcher's were later to become closely linked as both Thatcher and Loriks were involved in the founding of the Grain Terminal Association; Thatcher would for many years be the cooperative's manager.)

The rhetoric of the radicals, in regard to the New Deal, was fiery, to say the least. Milo Reno, at one point, accused Franklin Roosevelt of having had "wonderful courage to violate every pledge that he made in his campaign." The focus of many radical attacks was Secretary of Agriculture Henry Wallace and the New Deal "Brain Trust."

Both the radical and moderate groups had lobbyists in Washington for a time. The radical program included cost of production legislation and the Frazier-Lemke bill to refinance farm indebtedness—both of which were endorsed by Loriks in his speeches of the 1930s. The more moderate group was an active supporter of the New Deal farm legislation.

Though the Farmers Union conflict was really about the New Deal, the disagreements were often described in terms of the respective attitudes over cooperatives. The Farmers Union triangle is cooperation, education, and legislation, and much of the ongoing debate over the years has been over how to divide the emphasis in this triangle. The moderates in the 1930s thought that Simpson and his followers over-emphasized legislation at the expense of the other two sides.

Actually, both sides believed in all three parts of the triangle, Crampton said. Crampton also said that both the proposed solutions of the radicals were extreme, as well as their attitudes toward their more moderate opponents. "This became crucial in preventing any mending of the breach."

A climax came in 1936, when national secretary E.E. Kennedy, also editor of the *National Union Farmer,* tried to swing the Union behind the third-party candidacy of William Lemke in the 1936 presidential election. Kennedy's support of Lemke, who was tied to Father Coughlin, violated the Union's long national precedent of at "least nominal non-partisanship." So the 1936 national convention ousted Kennedy, replacing him with a moderate. He later tried to have his successor recalled, and even passed out nominating petitions to various South Dakotans to help do this, a move of which Emil Loriks was critical.

By the time of the 1937 national convention, a compromise candidate, John Vesecky, of Kansas, was elected president, after Everson had announced at the South Dakota convention earlier in the fall that he was getting out of national union politics became of his health. Crampton said that Everson left Union politics permanently and that Kennedy tried to form a rival farm group.

Some twenty years after all this factionalism in the national Union, James Patton, who became national president in 1940, said, "We had factions going in all directions. We had factions within factions. And, consequently, when our organization could have most effectively served the interests of farm families . . . we could not agree among ourselves how to go about it."

As Thompson has already said, Loriks in the South Dakota context was probably more a moderate figure, although much of his rhetoric during the 1930s, as shall be seen shortly, might have tended to suggest radicalism on his part. At one point during all the excitement in the national and state levels, there was even a suggestion from the Montana secretary, Harold Brown, that Loriks run for national Union president. Brown, in his letter to Loriks making this suggestion, said that the suggestion came from M.W. Thatcher and himself. The letter ended, "From what I have heard of you, I am sure that you will take it as an honest endeavor to work out a solution for the dissension that has weakened our National Union during the last year."

A challenge to Emil Loriks' state presidency was building by the summer of 1937; one of Loriks' main opponents was national president Everson. While the two—Everson and Loriks—had apparently worked together closely in the early part of both their terms in their respective presidencies, by 1937 the picture had changed. Letter after letter in the Loriks papers, refers to Everson's anti-Loriks efforts. A July 1937 letter that Loriks wrote to National Farmers Union board member Morris Erickson, of North Dakota, said in part:

> By the way, I got it via the grapevine route that the National President is going to devote considerable time between now and our state convention to eliminate the president of his own state from the picture. He has already done some organization work along this line, ably assisted by one E.E. Kennedy and others. I feel highly complimented.

Erickson answered Loriks in August with these comments:

> It looks like you are going to have a fight on your hands in South Dakota. I am confident, judging from the Farmers Union members I have talked to in South Dakota, that you will come out on top without any great difficulty. I think it is a good thing that our mutual friend is spreading all the scurrilous, untruthful propaganda about you. He will then have played his hand, and you will know all the cards. Everything he has rumored is so obviously false that if it is brought up at the state convention, it will act as a boomerang when you reply.

In late August, Loriks invited Erickson to the state convention, October 12-14. This meant that both a national board member favorable to Loriks, and the national president, E.G. Everson, would be there.

During the late summer and early fall, Emil Loriks wrote to several persons about E.G. Everson's activities in opposing him. Loriks' words were hardly kind, as in this letter to J.G. Graves, the National Union secretary:

The national president seems to be on a rampage
of criticism and denunciation of the national board
actions in blocking some of his projects this year. It
is regrettable indeed that a man so highly honored
in our own organizations as he has been should
write his final chapter in the venom of hatred and
bitterness. We are mighty sorry he has gotten into
this deplorable physical and mental state, much to
be regretted in a man holding his high position.

At other points during that fall of 1937, Loriks wondered in
his letters if "Everson had a screw loose."

Loriks and Everson were still in communication by letter,
although the correspondence was not a happy one. Everson
wondered in a late September letter if Loriks had deliberately
scheduled him to speak at the South Dakota convention at a
time when most delegates would have already left. "Did you
anticipate that a large number would be gone by that time,"
Everson asked Loriks. In a letter to national vice president
John Vesecky, who was soon to become national president,
Loriks wrote that Everson had been invited for the second day,
"the high spot in our convention. . . . He is just naturally
suspicious that we're stealing the spotlight from him in some
way." In the middle of all the battle, Loriks wondered if "there
shouldn't be much of me left when the convention is over."

However, Loriks did, on at least one occasion that fall, make
it difficult for national president Everson. In a letter to Morris
Erickson, Loriks explained:

Guess I told you over the telephone about the
"shenanigan" I pulled on Ed by inviting him to
speak at a picnic on the date that I knew he would be
on NBC. Then I called him at Des Moines and told
him he would have to send someone else, and that
the people out here were demanding Morris
Erickson (which was the truth). They didn't want
Ed at all. Well, it worked, and he said you should
make this picnic at his authorization.

The same letter noted later, "Ed has been spending much
time in South Dakota organizing against me, so I understand.
It has been sort of an undercover operation, so I understand."

The South Dakota convention, October 12-14, in Huron

resulted in Emil Loriks' being resoundingly re-elected, by a three-to-one margin over Roy Brasell of Madison. The *Evening Huronite* reported that, "although pre-convention gossip had pointed to spirited opposition to Loriks and other Union officers in their bid for re-election, the incumbents were returned to office by a wide margin." Loriks was also elected as a delegate to the national convention a few weeks later, which convention was to make the crucial decision to elect the moderate John Vesecky of Kansas as national president, thereby ending the dominance of the more radical faction.

Everson spoke twice at the state convention, according to newspaper accounts. Everson used one of his speeches to announce his impending retirement from the National Union presidency, because of "poor health." Loriks was decribed as "popular" in the *Huronite* story telling of his re-election.

Surprisingly, Loriks' 1937 convention speech made no mention of the internal Union dispute and of the efforts to unseat him as president. Instead, it was an emotionally stirring speech, beginning with this question, "Shall we crucify mankind on the cross of profits, or can we save mankind through economic democracy?" In Bryanesque terms, later in the speech, Loriks said, "Those of you who have helped these days, *you* have carried the *cross*. You know what it is to wear a crown of thorns—You have tasted the bitter cup."

After attacking excesses of the profit system, Loriks made this assertion: "We have a right to ask the federal government for aid and assistance in times of great emergencies, such as drought and flood, and other catastrophes beyond our control. It is the duty of government to come to the aid and assistance of any area that is so stricken."

He then made the statement which probably best reflects what was his essentially moderate approach to the Farmers Union and his position in the struggle in both the South Dakota and National Farmers Union. "We believe that cooperation should be recognized as the primary program of the Farmers Union, and that legislation should be supplementary thereto. As we build economic strength, we shall build legislative strength." The balance of Emil Loriks' 1937 convention address was spent in discussing state and national Farmers Union positions and legislation, suggesting that in Loriks, the South Dakota Farmers Union had a leader who could skillfully blend both the cooperative and legislative components of the Union's program.

Emil Loriks' rhetoric during his term as state Farmers Union president reflects the ambivalence of the organization itself. On the one hand, Loriks could offer praise for the New Deal and for Roosevelt, and on the other, he could make pointed attacks on Roosevelt and on Henry Wallace, and make statements praising such anti-New Deal figures as Father Charles Coughlin and Senator Huey Long.

For example, in a 1934 WNAX radio speech, Loriks had called Roosevelt "misguided." But in the same year, he spoke favorably of Roosevelt's visit to neighboring North Dakota to see firsthand the drought conditions there. Also in 1934, Loriks said in a letter that he was pleased that the President had signed the Frazier-Lemke bill.

In 1937, the Farmers Union was one of the few groups supporting the President's plan to expand the Supreme Court. Loriks in the 1980s was to admit that that may have been a mistake. Even in his 1937 presidential address to the South Dakota Farmers Union, he had admitted, "We fumbled the ball on the Court issue!"

In May 1934, in the same WNAX speech referred to just above, Loriks had said of the President, "Roosevelt is being deceived, just as sure as Hoover was deceived, by those who are now posing as his friends." A few paragraphs later, Loriks asserted, "Roosevelt was going to dump these pirates of high finance, but they are still clinging to the ship of state like barnacles to an old hull. *The money changers are still in the temple.*" Later in the same speech, Loriks criticized Agriculture Secretary Wallace for having "completely reversed himself" on the cost of production idea. Another speech of July 1934 also praised both Father Coughlin and Huey Long. He pronounced himself "impatient" with Roosevelt for not doing enough. The attacks continued in 1935 when Loriks called Wallace "high and mighty."

A very curious Loriks speech is his "early eulogy" of Huey Long, given on Loriks' regular radio time after Loriks had gotten word of Long's being shot, but before the death was confirmed. Loriks began by noting that Long had been scheduled to address the South Dakota Farmers Union convention later that year in October. The September 9 Loriks speech said, "Is the assassin's bullet, the cross or the hemlock ever going to be the reward for faithful service to humanity?" Loriks compared

Long to Socrates, to Jesus Christ and to Abraham Lincoln. Loriks called Long, the "most mis-represented, maligned and persecuted of statesmen today by the powerful interests that rule this nation, because he dared to attack the evils at their source," and said that he had "been shot down in cold blood."

At first glance, this eulogy might seem an incredible speech about one widely regarded by many as a demagogue, although not all historians, even at this point, share that view. Many have pointed to Long's accomplishments as Louisiana governor when he built miles and miles of roads and made improvements in the state's educational system. In speaking of the Long address fifty years later, Loriks defended it to a degree, saying that conditions in the country in the 1930s were very desperate, that Long seemed to offer some hope, and that he praised Long on the basis of his accomplishments as governor of Louisiana. "Long really performed in his day." Loriks' comments continued. "Huey was a spellbinder on the platform, and he had more 'guts' than any public official of his time to deal with the problems of his state and its people in the most tragic economic era of our history." Loriks also said that "in normal times, Long wouldn't have been possible." "Our eulogy of Huey was mainly through his record as governor of Louisiana and his support of what we fought for."

Actually, the Loriks speech makes considerably more sense for the last reason mentioned, the support that Long had given various farm groups in the 1930s. There was a somewhat uneasy relationship between the agrarians and Long, with each side seeking to gain something from the relationship. Long had addressed an April 1935 Farm Holiday meeting in Des Moines, speaking to a crowd estimated at anywhere from 10,000 to 18,000. Milo Reno had introduced Long as "the hero whom God in His goodness has vouchsafed to his children to save us from Roosevelt, Wallace, Tugwell and the rest of the traitors."

Even though some Farmers Union elements were to be involved in third party politics in 1936, Emil Loriks and the South Dakota Union were not. Loriks later said that he did not recall any active third party support from South Dakota for William Lemke. By that time, there was a movement in the direction of a more moderate stance at the national level.

In his many conversations with the author from 1982 until the time of his death in late 1985, Loriks was to emphasize his almost total reverence for Franklin Roosevelt. During Roosevelt's post-inauguration visit to South Dakota in 1933, Loriks was with a group that met with the President for an hour, an event that he remembered as "the thrill of a lifetime." Loriks noted that Roosevelt "promised immediate action by calling Congress into session for action to deal with the Depression."

But as has been demonstrated from the Loriks letters and speeches, Loriks did not fully support Roosevelt in the 1930s, especially in the early part, although he later came to regard Roosevelt in almost reverential terms, and was, in fact, part of the NBC telecast at the time of FDR's 100th birthday.

One other strain of Emil Loriks' 1930s rhetoric and the Farmers Union position of the era should be noted—the strong anti-war stance. Crampton has already been cited as saying that one of the four strands of the Union's ideology was pacifism.

In the 1930s, war clouds were gathering over Europe as Mussolini and Hitler made threatening moves. By the end of the decade, the Union was to move into the eventual mainstream that supported American involvement in World War II, but this was not the Union position in the 1930s. Many Loriks speeches of the 1930s criticized "those who would move us to war." Major portions of Emil Loriks' 1935 presidential address at the state Farmers Union convention dealt with the war threat. "Our expression on the subject of *war* should be courageous, bold and emphatic. *Let us keep America out of war!*" He referred to himself and to other Great War veterans as remembering the horrors of war, but said that "a new generation of mothers' sons has grown up, however, since the last war."

Loriks viewed the activities of Hitler and Mussolini in Europe in these terms: "Capitalism's unquenchable thirst for profit seeks to quench itself through territorial aggrandizement and expansion at the expense of weaker nations. *The world is again plunging into the seething cauldron of war.*" A bit later in the same speech, speaking of World War I, "We sent the flower of America's manhood three thousand miles across the waters to kill our brothers across the sea, all for *The House of Morgan.*"

The Farmers Union was hardly alone in its 1930s isolationist stance; this was a position shared by political liberals and conservatives.

Emil Loriks' presidency of the South Dakota Farmers Union occurred in the depths of the Great Depression and its resultant agrarian unrest. He became president sooner than expected because of the death of John Simpson, and quickly moved to devote himself full-time to the Union's activities, quitting both his Farm Holiday position and the South Dakota Senate.

One of the South Dakota Farmers Union's greatest accomplishments—the successful lobbying for the enactment of a gold severance tax, occurred during Loriks' term and in large part because of his efforts and those of other Farmers Union leaders, like Oscar Fosheim (strategically a member of the House, during the 1935 ore tax battle.) Loriks brought to the Union a mature viewpoint in presenting and lobbying for legislation that the Union wanted and knowing when compromise was indicated. He was also able to improve relations with the rival Farm Bureau.

Loriks in some ways brought together the concerns of both the moderate and radical elements in the Union, and in so doing, withstood a challenge to his leadership that was largely orchestrated by his immediate predecessor in the South Dakota presidency, Everson, by then national president. In his somewhat emotional rhetoric, Emil Loriks could appeal to the desire of radicals for more action by the Roosevelt administration. But in his deeds and careful approach, Loriks carefully crafted a legislative program and lobbied for that program. This blending of approaches was in large part made possible because Loriks was himself a former legislator, and still had many good legislative contacts, many of them Union members. Loriks stressed the need for reforming the capitalistic system through the building of cooperatives, and was later to spend twenty-seven years practicing that as a board member and eventually president of the Grain Terminal Association, the world's large grain marketing cooperative.

The Loriks tenure as president of the South Dakota Farmers Union can be seen as fruitful years for both him and his organization. His work as Union president also helped him develop the skills and interest he would later use as a Congressional candidate, a New Deal farm agency administrator, national secretary of the Farmers Union, and a GTA leader and spokesman.

CHAPTER IV

1938 Congressional Campaign

In 1938 Emil Loriks would turn forty-three. He was well established, both in the public service realm and in his family life. His daughter, Ruth Ann, born in 1930, would turn eight in this year. His family farm operation was one of considerable magnitude, an operation for which he had been responsbile following the death of his father in 1928. At one time the Loriks operation, in the days of horses, covered twelve sections of productive Kingsbury County land. In addition to the usual crops of corn, oats, barley and flax, Loriks at times fed as many as one hundred Herefords and also raised hogs. There were usually a small number of milk cows on the farm as well, with the Loriks family selling some of the cream. Ruth Loriks, her daughter recalled, raised chickens, sometimes as many as one thousand at a time, and had a thriving egg business—like many farm wives of her era.

Especially from the mid-1930s on, when he became state Farmers Union president, Loriks was away from home for great amounts of time, so the day-to-day operation of the farm fell to Ruth, and also to her father, Charles Dahlen, who lived until 1949. After the death of Ruth's mother in 1938, the elder Dahlen made his home with the Loriks family.

Given all the public service background, and also the suggestions that he should seek a political office—coming from both public and private quarters—it is not surprising that in 1938 Loriks finally did seek a higher governmental office. In 1937, Loriks and the moderates had established firm control of the South Dakota Farmers Union, a step the national Union completed late in the same year with the election of John Vesecky as national president. In a sense, it was time to move on.

Emil Loriks was one of six Democratic candidates in the May 1938 primary. The party strategy may well have been to run that many candidates so that no one would have a winning majority and the state party convention would choose the party nominee. An April 14, 1938, letter to E.L. Oliver of the

Emil Loriks at harvest time.

Photo courtesy of Ruth Ann Carlson

The Loriks barn and silo.

Photo by the author

Labor Nonpartisan League made just that comment. "Six candidates in the race for Congress obviously to block anyone getting 35 percent and to throw the nomination into the State Convention controlled by the political machine."

Loriks apparently did not campaign in the primary race. In the letter just mentioned, he said, "Personally, I am not participating in the Primary Campaign, and it will just have to take its course."

A letter written the same day to W.R. Ronald, editor of the *Mitchell Daily Republic,* thanked Ronald for his editorial support during the primary race. "A word of gratitude and appreciation for the fine editorial support of my candidacy for Congress. I cannot personally participate in this Primary Campaign, so my nomination rests entirely in the hands of my friends and you have contributed materially."

Not all of Emil Loriks' Farmers Union associates were happy about his entry into partisan politics, feeling that he was needed more as a farm leader. This view was clearly expressed to Loriks in a letter of April 16, 1938, from A.W. Ricker of St. Paul, editor of the *Farmers Union Herald.* "First of all, I want to give you a scolding for permitting yourself to become a candidate for Congress. . . . The common verdict was 'here's another good man gone wrong.' "

Ricker continued, "You see, we have built great hopes for you as a farm leader in South Dakota. When you cease to be a farm leader and become a Congressman, then you are just a politician. You might, and I believe you would, make a wonderful Congressman, but who is to take your place as South Dakota's farm leader?"

Ricker did end the letter by saying that if Loriks' decision to run was final, "then of course we are going to be just as warmly for you as a Congressman as we are for you as state president of the South Dakota Farmers Union. We shall just feel grieved and let it go at that."

Much to everyone's surprise, Loriks did win the May 3 primary outright. Loriks' 19,701 votes represented more than 38 percent of the total 51,249 votes cast in the Democratic primary. Running second in the primary race was Arthur Bennett of Milbank, who polled 11,969 votes, while the other four candidates each polled in the 4,000 to 5,000 vote range. In his own Kingsbury County the victory was even more emphatic—his 458 votes were more than the total of the other five candidates combined. Thirty years later, writing about that campaign in a letter to Chamberlain attorney John F. Lindley, Loriks observed, "When I won the nomination against this galaxy of candidates without making one single primary appearance, I found that two of my primary opponents went over to the other side and supported Mundt. My contest with Mundt was fairly close but I have always felt that the primary blew my chances."

The 1938 Congressional campaign in South Dakota's First District between Emil Loriks and Karl Mundt has been examined carefully in an article by SDSU history professor John Miller. His article in the summer 1982 *Heritage of the Great Plains* is entitled "McCarthyism Before McCarthy: the 1938 Election in South Dakota;" the title aptly reflects what kind of campaign it was. This narrative of that campaign is drawn primarily from Miller's excellent study, as well as from newspaper clippings of that year and letters in the Loriks papers.

The 1938 South Dakota election featured Loriks' fellow South Dakota Farmers Union leader Oscar Fosheim running for governor on the Democratic ticket against Republican Harlan J. Bushfield. Conservative Democrat Tom Berry, having won in the Democratic primary over Fred Hildebrandt, ran for the senate against Republican Chan Gurney. In the Second Congressional District, Democrat Theo Werner was running against Republican Francis Case.

The Republican Congressional nominee, Karl Mundt, won his right to compete in the fall election without primary opposition. Mundt, although he had never before held elective of-

A Loriks bumper sticker from the 1938 Congressional campaign.

Sticker found in the Loriks papers

fice, was a well-known figure in the state, and in the 1936 election, had only narrowly lost the First District race to Democratic Congressman Fred Hildebrandt, losing by only 2,570 votes. Holder of an M.A. from Columbia Teachers College, Mundt had taught speech at Eastern Normal, Emil Loriks' alma mater, and was founder of the National Forensic League. He was active in many organizations like Kiwanis and the Masonic orders.

Professor Miller views this 1938 race and, in fact, the whole 1938 campaign in South Dakota as "evidence of how anti-communism was utilized for partisan political ends during the years before 1950" (when the late Senator Joseph McCarthy of Wisconsin made his first major anti-communist speech). Mundt in his thirty-four years in the House and Senate built a reputation as an outspoken anti-communist.

Right after Loriks' primary victory, fellow Union leader Morris Erickson, national board member from North Dakota, had written:

> I am somewhat at a loss to determine whether to offer you my condolences or congratulations on your nomination for Congress. In a lot of respects, I can almost envy you for the opportunity that will be yours if the election turns out all right this fall. On the other hand, the loss to the South Dakota Farmers Union will be serious.

Loriks moved to resign his post as state Union president, to be free to conduct his campaign. In a May 25 letter to fellow South Dakota Union leader Enoch Hofstad, he discussed his plans to resign, setting a July date. Loriks also indicated in this letter that he knew what sort of campaign lay ahead. "Somehow, I feel this Congress fight will be the toughest proposition I ever got into and I think your encouragement had much to do with my getting in the fight."

A little later, speaking of Karl Mundt, who by early June had already had coverage in the Republican *Argus-Leader* of one of his anti-communist speeches, Loriks added, "It would be interesting to know just what contributions he has made during his lifetime toward any solution of economic injustices, besides being a payroller of the State; also how one who never served under the colors either in *war* or other emergency can wrap himself in the flag and hurl un-American epithets at others. Such super-patriots! Apologists say, 'He was too young and that Bushfield [GOP governor nominee] was too old!' They were neither too young nor too old to volunteer! They must be just the right age now!" A further Loriks comment was, "Their battle cry now is fight 'radicalism' in any form, crusaders against symptoms rather than causes."

As had been true the year before in the Farmers Union presidency contest, Ed Everson was one of Emil Loriks' leading adversaries in the 1938 Congressional campaign. The Loriks campaign obtained a copy of an Everson letter of July 1, 1938, written on national Farmers Union letterhead listing Everson as president (though he had not been since November 1937) which revealed his strategy. The Everson letter, written to someone in Vermillion, read, "The thought just occurred to me that it would be good politics on the part of my many Republican friends and would no doubt be the means of securing votes away from Fosheim and Loriks if Bushfield would assure a few of the Farm Union leaders who are four square . . . that he would make me his Secretary of Agriculture if elected."

Incredibly, for those who remember Karl Mundt as a conservative Republican lawmaker, in 1938 he "insisted upon being labelled a liberal Republican," according to John Miller. Mundt said, "I am a liberal Republican who wants government to go forward the American way." This was a shrewd campaign stance in that he could appeal both to disenchanted Democrats, unhappy with the New Deal, and progressive Republicans. Mundt's campaign slogan that year, and throughout his career, was "A Fair Chance for a Free People." Mundt appeared to be sympathetic to the cost of production for farmers, and was in favor of federal aid to education, and also sent out sympathetic feelers to the elderly for their vote.

While Mundt was making public statements that emphasized his progressive side, privately, Miller said, he was working to shape a state Republican platform that would undercut the appeal of Emil Loriks and Oscar Fosheim to rural voters. He supported various farm programs while attacking Loriks and Fosheim as radicals. Everson, in the words of Miller, in working with the Mundt campaign, "vented his spleen against Emil Loriks."

Everson traveled around the state attacking Loriks and Fosheim and the New Deal. Another player in the campaign was former National Farmers Union Secretary E.E. Kennedy, who had been ousted from his national office after being involved in the third party candidacy of William Lemke in 1936. Another Union leader, John Batcheller, a past president of the South Dakota Union before E.G. Everson, also came out against Loriks and Fosheim.

One of the hidden issues in the campaign, which Mundt did not raise directly, but let others raise for him, was over whether Emil Loriks had been a paid "collaborator" for the New Deal Department of Agriculture. This charge had also been used against Loriks in 1937 during the campaign to defeat him as Farmers Union state president. What Loriks had done was to serve briefly as a consultant, but the Mundt campaign used the term "collaborator" and suggested that this would serve "as a whole array of red flags for someone." In various letters that fall, Mundt said of this strategy, "I could transmit this information in its specific form to certain places where it could do me just a whole lot of good between now and election time. I do not expect to use it myself in any way but by giving this information to the proper Farm Union leaders it would be very beneficial."

Miller said that Mundt used the same strategy of indirection "to undermine his opponent's credibility and to cast doubt on his character and public record." In the campaign Loriks was vulnerable for a couple of reasons: his New Deal leanings and his identification with several allegedly radical or un-American groups. Further, Loriks' one-time support of Robert M. LaFollete and Woodrow Wilson and his involvement with the Farmers Holiday and the Farmers Union made him suspect in many quarters.

And there were certainly ties between Loriks and labor, although this hardly would make him a radical. In 1937, while still Union president, Loriks had been invited to a progressive and liberal meeting in Huron. Loriks had also invited Albert Maag, president of the South Dakota Federation of Labor, to the 1937 state Farmers Union convention. But the biggest campaign issue was a December 1937 meeting in St. Paul, Minnesota, that Loriks and other Farmers Union leaders from neighboring states had attended. There was an agreement he signed to cooperate with Labor's Nonpartisan League, a CIO offshoot, in a joint legislative program for the following year. This issue was made even worse for Loriks by the fact that this

St. Paul meeting had been glowingly reported in the Communist Party's *Daily Worker*.

An undated and unlabeled newspaper editorial found in an Emil Loriks scrapbook said in part about this agreement with the CIO:

> South Dakotans are more than a little disturbed over the agreement which Emil Loriks, Democratic candidate for Congress in the First District, signed at St. Paul last December.
>
> According to this agreement, Loriks is obligated to vote in behalf of CIO legislation if he is elected to Congress.
>
> The question that naturally arises in the minds of South Dakotans is this: Do we want in Congress a man who will represent us, or one who is already alleged to divide his representation with a group such as the CIO?
>
> The tactics of the CIO are not the kind in which South Dakotans believe. They have faith in a government of law and order, not in one in which organized groups defy the law.
>
> So today the choice for Congress in the First District lies between a man who is willing to support the principles of the CIO, and one who has sharply attacked them.
>
> Karl Mundt, the Republican candidate, has made his position clear. He believes in law and order and will represent South Dakota, not the CIO, if he is elected.

This editorial was almost mild compared with others. An *Argus Leader* editorial two weeks before the election noted Loriks' signing of the Labor agreement and Communist leader Earl Browder's endorsement of that pact. The editorial noted Loriks' participation "in an agreement that the national secretary of the Communist party now heralds as 'one of our most cherished ambitions.' The *Argus Leader* does not believe that Loriks is a Communist. It does maintain, however, that his radical approach to public problems is assisting the CIO, and in turn, the Communist party."

Miller described the *Argus Leader*'s actions in the 1938 campaign in this way: "Throughout the campaign, the *Argus*

Leader was the most influential and one of the worst offenders of fairness and common decency in its completely unsubtle efforts to associate Loriks and Fosheim and Congressman Fred Hildebrandt with the Communists." Miller further pointed out that the *Argus Leader*'s influence "was statewide and its editorials were widely reproduced in dailies and weeklies."

Some of the *Argus Leader*'s statements included the following:

> Governmental radicalism is a major issue in the South Dakota campaign and let no one forget it. . . . They are stirring class hatred. They are encouraging dependency. . . . Bear in mind that the Democratic candidates have received the endorsement of the Communists and other subversive groups and ask yourself why. What do they expect from them? Why do they favor them? Why do they say they will vote for them? The answers are plain. They believe their subversive causes will be advanced to a greater degree through a Democratic rather than a Republican victory. They are interested in dissension, in strife, and in the destruction of American democracy.

Still another *Argus Leader* editorial said, "We are not saying that Loriks and Fosheim in fact are Communists." But it went on to say, "Candidates who endorse policies that are communistic in nature should not be surprised when they, in turn, receive the blessings of the Communists."

Miller pointed out what was perhaps the supreme irony of the campaign:

What made Loriks and Fosheim's programs communistic in the eyes of the conservatives, such as the *Argus Leader*'s editors, was their affinity for liberal and New Deal-type measures that used governmental power to promote the interests of farmers, laborers, the unemployed, and other special interest groups. Yet they did not hesitate to extol the candidacy of Karl Mundt, who advocated cost of production for farmers, federal aid for education, and increased pensions for the aged.

Given the attacks that the Republicans were making on Emil Loriks for his support of the New Deal, he could well have gotten into the campaign record some of his Farmers Union presidential speeches of 1934 and 1935 that had been highly critical of Secretary of Agriculture Wallace and even President Roosevelt.

In view of this barrage of criticism, it is not surprising that Loriks' November 1, 1938, political ad in the *Argus Leader* started with, "Loriks' Record for Americanism Speaks for Itself." The ad went on to say:

> The facts about Emil Loriks make the attempts to "smear" him despicable beyond expression.
>
> Loriks was only a boy when war was declared in 1917. He did not then—any more than he would now—sympathize with the professional politicians, profiteers and patrioteers who were largely responsible for dragging us into it.
>
> But—like thousands of farm boys—*he was there to be wounded when the time came.*
>
> Within three months he was in the service *as a buck private in the regular Army—a volunteer.*
>
> He served eighteen months. On his merits as a soldier, he won promotion to a commission as an aviator.
>
> He was the first commander of his post of the American Legion. He has been, is, and always will be the same kind of a square, straightforward, clean-cut fellow who willingly and simply does his duty—*rather than the kind who takes it out in spread eagle speeches.*
>
> It is almost beyond belief, that in the face of such a record, any attempt would be made to smear the Americanism of Emil Loriks.

One of the most ardent anti-communist spokesmen in South Dakota during the fall of 1938 was Arthur Bennett of Milbank, who had run second to Emil Loriks in the Democratic First District Congressional primary that spring. In 1936, Bennett had been the Union Party senatorial candidate and he was a supporter of the Townsend old age pension plan. Although Democratic leaders tried to silence Bennett, he persisted in alleging that the South Dakota Progressive Federation had been organized with communist money for the purpose of nominating Loriks, Fosheim and Hildebrandt (then First

District congressman who had lost the Democratic senatorial primary to Tom Berry). Bennett called the three, "not Democrats at heart but radical farmer-laborites." Bennett had printed and then distributed a four-page brochure that warned, "South Dakotans Wake Up—Tomorrow May Be Too Late!" The brochure featured a picture of Emil Loriks and fellow Farmers Union members signing the St. Paul pact, and then said, "Not at our front door does Communism raise its ugly and menacing head, but in its usual slinking, sinister, treacherous way—like a thief in the night—disguised as 'progress' to hide its ugly claws, it is attempting to slip in the back door, *right here in South Dakota*, and deprive us of everything we hold dear." One story which Bennett and his friends used to great impact in the campaign was that of Linn Gale, a Communist who had briefly been on the staff of Congressman Fred Hildebrandt before the Congressman became aware of his political leanings.

There were also a number of clergy involved in the anti-communist aspects of the 1938 campaign. Probably the best known was Father Hugh K. Wolf of Garretson who, although a registered Democrat, had established a cordial relationship with Karl Mundt. In a speech to the Sioux Falls Kiwanis Club during the campaign, Father Wolf asserted that Emil Loriks owed his re-election as state president of the Farmers Union "to the support of the communist bloc within that group." In addition, Wolf said, communist party funds "saved the day" for the recently organized South Dakota Progressive Voters organization by furnishing it funds when the treasury was at low ebb.

In the speech, Father Wolf referred to an alleged letter from a McCook County Farmers Union leader that referred to the Farmers Union situation. The writer of the letter said, "The communists were the only group I could get to rally to Loriks' support."

Still another newspaper clipping, undated and unidentified as to source, and found in the Loriks scrapbook, contains these allegations in referring to Emil Loriks having signed the pact with labor in St. Paul, "The name of Emil Loriks appears on the part of the Farmers Union. It quite definitely hooks Loriks up with communistic sympathizers and radicals."

Some of the rhetoric on Loriks' behalf was not exactly restrained either by the time the campaign reached its climax.

A letter saved by Loriks was written by J.B. Fulton of Sioux Falls and published in the Sioux City *Tribune*. In referring to the McCook County Farmers Union leader whose statements were forming a major part of Republican efforts, the letter stated, "Yes, the speaker was prominent all right, but not as a farmer or Farm Union man of McCook County, but he allegedly bore the reputation of a moonshiner and bootlegger in South Dakota during the hectic days of prohibition . . . ."

Although Mundt mostly had others carrying out the anti-communist campaign for him, just before the election, he was more direct. At a rally in Sisseton, he said that "the Communist party of South Dakota is now openly holding political rallies to defeat me and I accept their opposition cheerfully." Without referring to the Democrats, Mundt said, "I have been fighting the un-Christian and un-American doctrines of Communism in speeches and articles for over ten years and I shall continue to openly and honestly oppose them in spite of the added opposition it produces; in fact, I am glad they recognize in me such a sincere opportunity that they are now holding meetings in an effort to defeat me."

Even the House Un-American Activities Committee, which was chaired by Representative Martin Dies of Texas, became a factor in the South Dakota campaign in 1938. On October 22, the GOP state chairman, J.D. Coon, along with the major Republican candidates including Mundt, asked the committee to investigate charges of Communist political activity in South Dakota. The Republicans wanted the committee to look into the charges of Communism in South Dakota and "to determine whether, through the Progressive Labor Federation, the Communists were influencing the Democratic candidates." Hans Ustrud, the secretary of the South Dakota Progressive Federation, and a former lieutenant governor under Tom Berry, invited the committee into the state to investigate his organization and also to look at "the un-American activities of the Homestake mine," which Ustrud said dominated the Republican party in selecting candidates and winning elections.

Emil Loriks said in conversations with this writer in the early 1980s that he privately challenged Karl Mundt that they both go before the Un-American Activities Committee, but nothing ever happened. As Miller wrote, the committee did fail to act on the Republican request and the committee went into recess.

Miller wrote that Karl Mundt actually anticipated defeat as the campaign neared its end. He desperately requested funds from the Republican Congressional Committee, which provided him $2,000 of the $3,500 total he spent during the campaign, definitely a low-budget operation in light of 1980s' $1 million Congressional campaign.

Emil Loriks probably spent even less on his campaign, although no direct reports can be found in his papers, and his family at this point does not know what he may have spent on the campaign. The Loriks race was being watched nationally by the Democratic party; there are several letters in the Loriks files from National Democratic Committee chairman James Farley asking for information on developments in the South Dakota campaign, and also a letter after the election asking for an analysis.

When the votes were counted in November, Emil Loriks and the entire Democratic ticket lost. Loriks polled 46 percent of the votes and Fosheim also polled 46 percent in the gubernatorial race. Miller wrote, "The swing to the right was obvious to everyone, but in South Dakota that should have been less surprising than was the continued strength demonstrated by the Democrats."

Throughout the nation there was a tide against the Democrats. The Republicans picked up eighty-one seats in the House of Representatives, won eight in the Senate and captured a net of thirteen governorships. Although the election cannot be clearly seen as a rejection of the New Deal, historian William Leuchtenburg wrote, it was a "heavy blow" for the Roosevelt coalition.

In his article, Miller asked whether the Mundt and Republican campaign strategy was a "sophisticated and cynical effort to manipulate the campaign." Miller concluded, "It appears more accurate to say that the party, frustrated after almost six years of Democratic rule in Washington, was desperately grasping at any opportunity that promised electoral victory."

Miller wrote that the popularity of the Communist issue was both political and also a reflection of the climate of opinion of that time. The world was a very uneasy place in the fall of 1938; during September and October, the Munich crisis in Europe was dominating the headlines. There were severe

economic and social dislocations in the entire country. As
Miller wrote:

> As farms blew away during the dust storms, cat-
> tle perished in the drought, people went on relief,
> and to work for the WPA, farm sales were blocked
> by angry farmers, dictators raved in Europe, and
> power concentrated in Washington, and it was no
> wonder that people became alarmed with what was
> going on and were worried about what would hap-
> pen next.

Nor was the Communist issue totally without substance.
William Leuchtenburg wrote that beginning in 1935, the Communists had de-emphasized their revolutionary aims to enter
with American liberals into a common or popular front against
fascism. There was also a "Popular Front" operating in farm
circles, according to Lowell K. Dyson. In the mid-1930s the
Communists had made efforts to join in activities of the Farm
Holiday and the Farmers Union in various locations in the
United States. The Kennedy-Everson or ideological wing of
the National Farmers Union, finally driven from power at the
Union's 1937 national convention, was seen by its adversaries
in the Union as "fascists." The cooperative wing, whose
leadership included A.W. Ricker and M.W. Thatcher, which
came into Union power in 1936 and 1937, was considered as
"Communist" in some quarters. There continued throughout
1936-37 within the Union an unsure battle between the
Kennedy-Father Coughlin interests and the cooperator-
Populist Front group. Dyson says that the Farmers Union was
no more dominated by Communists than the real powers
(Ricker, Thatcher, Glen Talbot of North Dakota, and James
Patton, later president) would allow. But it could be viewed as
a Popular Front organization because its leaders on principle
opposed both war and fascism.

The resultant edginess and even fear in people "made them
more receptive to arguments based on fear," Miller said. This
made it possible for the Communist issue to dominate the 1938
South Dakota campaign. Mundt also appropriated, skillfully,
some liberal themes and Loriks concentrated on agricultural
problems and on defending the New Deal, although he did not
and had not totally supported the Roosevelt policies.

Miller finds the role that the Communist issue really played in South Dakota "difficult to determine." It may have influenced a few voters' decisions, but "No doubt it did more to reinforce previously established positions than to change those decisions. It convinced those who were already convinced. No big swing occurred in 1938. The unfortunate outcome, however, was that red-baiting seemed to be a useful tactic for winning elections."

Both the state chair and the vice chair of the South Dakota Democratic party wrote to Emil Loriks after his defeat to offer their sympathy. Mrs. P.L. Crowlie, vice chair, wrote, "I am still shocked over the results of the election. I feel that we had the best candidates that the Democratic party has offered to the people of South Dakota. The only explanation that I can give is that the trend was away from the New Deal Program." A.W. Powell, Democratic chairman, also saw the defeat in terms of loss of the farm vote.

Fellow Farmers Union leader Enoch Hofstad, in a long letter written in December to Loriks, said, "The people did not want a continuance of the present farm program." Saying that he did not realize farmers' strong feelings after the election, he wrote, "I certainly would have advised you to repudiate the statements made that you were pledged to support the present farm program. I did not hardly believe [sic] that claim when I heard it made—was it really true that you were pledged to support it?"

Hofstad went on to comment about the Republicans' having used the cost of production concept in their campaign, having "worked it for all it was worth. We therefore found the incongruous situation of Republican candidates benefiting from the Farmers Union plan—when, logically, the Democratic candidates, having been Farmers Union officials, should have had whatever benefit that plank could bring."

So it was probably the farm situation and South Dakotans' unhappiness with New Deal farm policy and the skillful use of anti-Communist campaign strategy that were crucial in Emil Loriks' loss to Karl Mundt in 1938.

After such a bitter and personal campaign, when his very loyalty to his country was questioned, Loriks might have been forgiven had he left public service. He might even have been forgiven had he been bitter about the campaign. But neither of these developments happened. Emil Loriks went on to serve the public, and especially agriculture, in other major ways, including serving as a state, and later, regional administrator, for the Farm Security Administration. In addition, he continued to be active in the Farmers Union, serving just over three years in the early 1940s as national secretary treasurer. But his real commitment was to be to the Grain Terminal Association where he not only led in the cooperative movement, but developed and cultivated important political connections through the GTA's lobbying in Washington, D.C., on farm policy issues.

Miller, in discussing Emil Loriks as a personality at a fall 1984 meeting, said that Emil Loriks, unlike many other agrarian farm leaders of the 1930s, "never became bitter or turned inward." Ed Everson, after leaving the national Farmers Union presidency in 1937 and his anti-Loriks campaign efforts in 1938, left Union matters, and apparently turned sour, Miller said. Other Democrats took defeat hard. "But Emil Loriks has always been cheerful."

Loriks probably agreed with the assessment offered by James Farley in a letter to Loriks two weeks after the election.

> I, of course, was extremely sorry when the result on Election Day indicated your defeat. I realize full well the splendid campaign conducted by you, and I was hoping you would win. However, it apparently wasn't in the cards. But may I suggest to you that you not feel at all discouraged about it, because you conducted a good fight, and I know you put every effort for yourself as well as for your associates.

On a more personal level, at least one member of the Loriks family was happy that her father did not win the election. Ruth Ann Loriks Carlson later recalled that she did not want to move to Washington, being just eight the fall of the election. And besides, Emil Loriks' defeat may have opened the many other doors of service to him, doors that he confidently entered throughout the rest of his career. But one does ask what sort of Congressman Loriks might have been, and how different his life and career would have been, had he won that 1938 election.

On November 9, Loriks sent this note to Karl Mundt. "Congratulations on your election and your opportunity to serve South Dakota and the nation."

Mundt wrote back a gracious note on November 11. "Thank you for your note of congratulations which has just arrived. It was a great fight and you were a worthy opponent." Speaking prophetically, he said, "I hope we can come to know each other better in the years to come." Mundt added, "I am sure neither of us are as bad as we were sometimes described by our respective groups of friends, and I hope that you drop in at Madison whenever you are through this way as I would like to have the opportunity to become a better friend of yours."

Mundt also promised to work with the Farmers Union on legislation. "I shall be happy to join with you and your organization at any time in any fight which works to the permanent advantage of South Dakota and the nation."

CHAPTER V

Emil Loriks: Cooperative Builder, 1939-1957

The nineteen years between Emil Loriks' loss to Karl Mundt in 1938 and his assuming the presidency of the Grain Terminal Association of 1957 can be viewed as his time of being a builder of cooperatives. There are three intertwining strands to his career during those years. One was his involvement with the GTA, which he helped to found, and whose board of directors he officially joined in December 1940. Another was as a state and, later, regional administrator for the New Deal's Farm Security Administration, this occurring in 1940-42. A major concern of Loriks' work in the FSA was in helping to start and strengthen farm cooperatives.

The final strain was his continuing involvement in the Farmers Union, at both state and national levels. Five years after being elected to the national Farmers Union board in 1937, he was elected secretary-treasurer, a position he held until early 1946.

All the while, Loriks took great pride in his membership in the South Dakota Farmers Union. During the 1940s he prided himself as being a "foot soldier" in the state Union, but by the early 1950s, he again held an official position as an administrative assistant in the state office, serving in a variety of roles including editor of the *South Dakota Union Farmer* and director of organization. He left this Farmers Union position in the fall of 1956. During the time he served in the state office, he lived in Huron at least during the week, returning to his Kingsbury County farm on weekends.

Loriks firmly believed in cooperatives and the philosophy which underlay cooperatives. Excerpts from undated notes for a speech found in the Loriks papers characterize that belief. The notes included these comments:

> Cooperative—neighbor helping neighbor in the American and the Christian way. It takes many

hands working together to preserve our American way of family farm life.

Cooperatives are neighbor helping neighbor in business. Cooperatives are democracy in business—*economic democracy*. Without economic democracy, political democracy cannot long survive. Cooperatives help diffuse the ownership of things among a greater number of people.

It cannot be emphasized too strongly or too frequently that the soul of the cooperative movement is not personal profit or money profit, but a Christian and neighborly interest and concern for the common good and the welfare of each member of society.

Coops are the engines of democracy.

GTA Founder and Leader

The Grain Terminal Association did not suddenly emerge in the late 1930s, but was the result of many years of adverse marketing conditions and of earlier efforts to develop such a cooperative marketing system.

Early in the twentieth century, the grain market was essentially controlled by railroads, bankers, and the grain companies. In 1908, farmers organized the Equity Cooperative Exchange in an attempt to control the market cooperatively. In 1914, the Equity formed the St. Paul Grain Exchange, and in 1916, it built a terminal elevator on the Mississippi River in St. Paul.

The Equity failed and in 1926 the Farmers Union Terminal Association was formed to pick up where the Equity had failed. The Farmers Union Terminal Association worked to get uniform inspection regulations and honest weighing at local and terminal elevators. During the Depression, the Terminal Association aligned itself with the quasi-governmental Farmers National Grain Corporation. The Farmers Union Terminal Association became the Grain Terminal Association, beginning with a formal incorporation in 1936, and the official start of business on June 1, 1938.

The key figure in the founding of the GTA and in its operations until 1962 was M.W. "Bill" Thatcher. The strong-minded and often controversial Thatcher, born in 1882 in Indiana, was a city boy who had many farm relatives. After taking a business and finance major in college, Thatcher worked as an accountant in Chicago, and later after having a couple of stints in Minneapolis, he eventually moved there because he liked it so well. In 1920, he went to North Dakota to work in Bismarck and found himself caught up in the Nonpartisan League and in cooperative work. He later became manager of the GTA forerunner, the Equity Coop Exchange.

Thatcher, along with North Dakota Farmers Union president C.C. Talbott, and cooperative editor A.W. Ricker, was part of the Northwest Organizing Committee of the Farmers Union, founded in 1927. This committee, whose purpose was described by John Crampton as promoting the organization of the Union in the Upper Midwest, provided a nucleus for the moderates in the ongoing struggle in the 1930s between the moderate and radical factions.

Thatcher worked in Washington, D.C., from 1931 to 1937 as the lobbyist for the Farmers National Grain Corporation, and at the same time was also a lobbyist for the moderate wing of the Farmers Union.

In 1937, Thatcher met with Upper Midwest Farmers Union leaders from Minnesota, Montana, and the Dakotas, including Loriks, to lay the groundwork for the new GTA. In late December, Thatcher met with President Franklin D. Roosevelt and gained his approval. Roosevelt directed Agriculture Secretary Henry Wallace to "try to work out" the Thatcher proposal. There was this close government connection for several reasons. One was that the GTA, at its start of business in June 1938, took over the 121 local associations which had been in the quasi-governmental Farmers National Grain Corporation. In addition, $300,000 long-term money from the Farm Credit Administration's Farm Board Revolving Fund helped start the GTA, as did $900,000 of short-term operating credit.

In 1939, through its organization and reorganization of 129 local associations, GTA farmer members gave notes totaling $307,000 to the Farm Security Administration. There was also start-up capital for the GTA of $30,000 from the Farmers Union Central Exchange (later CENEX), which the Farmers Union Terminal Association had helped start in 1931. By the end of 1939, there were 250 local associations in the GTA.

In its first year, the GTA handled seventeen million bushels

of grain and netted savings of $144,000. A related develop-
ment was the organization, in 1939, of the National Federation
of Grain Cooperatives, with Thatcher being its first, and longtime president. This all-encompassing group had as its goal to
stop the Commodity Credit Corporation's entry into the grain
business. The Federation presidency was to give Thatcher an
even wider forum as the years went on.

Emil Loriks officially joined the GTA board of directors on
December 10, 1940. But he had sat in on board meetings in an
unofficial capacity since the 1939 annual meeting, which had
authorized an increase in the number of GTA directors so as to
give South Dakota a member. A letter to Loriks in early 1940
from the GTA president explained that "it was agreed between ourselves, representatives of the Farm Security Administration and others from South Dakota that you would sit
in as an ex-officio member of the board."

In the early 1940s, GTA built a large terminal elevator in
Superior, Wisconsin, with a capacity of nearly five million
bushels, and the tallest and fastest elevator built to that date.
Also in 1941, GTA started its feed business and its *GTA
Digest.*

Thatcher, whom the *Minneapolis Morning Tribune* described in a story on December 22, 1946, as "a leader in the
cooperative movement and in efforts to obtain price security to
insure the future of farmers," maintained very close ties with
the Roosevelt Administration in the GTA's early years. Even

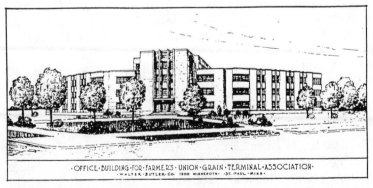

·OFFICE·BUILDING·FOR·FARMER'S·UNION·GRAIN·TERMINAL·ASSOCIATION·
·WALTER·BUTLER·CO· 1300 MINNESOTA· ·ST·PAUL·MINN·

**The architect's drawing of the GTA Headquarters Building,
dedicated December 11, 1946.**

Drawing from Loriks Papers

competitors to the always-controversial Thatcher were quoted in the *Tribune* story as saying of the GTA, "it is an extremely effective marketing organization. They say much of its success is based on Bill Thatcher and his ability to sell ideas." One of the GTA's key rivals in the realms of ideas was the National Tax Equity Association, whose claim was that coops, like the GTA, got "special" privileges. An ongoing fight over the years was about whether cooperative patronage dividends should be taxed as income.

Much of the GTA's thrust in the early years was political, a thrust reflected in the various letters that Loriks wrote to political leaders and in the letters back and forth between GTA manager Thatcher and GTA board member Loriks. Both Loriks and Thatcher wrote numerous letters to senators and congressmen of both political parties to urge full parity prices for farmers and favorable treatment for cooperatives.

In letters back and forth between Loriks and Thatcher, Loriks always started his letters, "Dear Mr. Thatcher," at the same time Thatcher was writing "Dear Emil."

The early GTA years, through the 1940s, were also times of building and acquisition, with the addition of numerous elevators and the development of a lumber business, later known as Great Plains Supply. The GTA also moved into the public relations arena more and more, reaching beyond its own membership with a radio program.

Loriks was apparently a key speaker at the 1943 GTA annual meeting, which had to resolve a sticky issue involving the ouster of two board members who had, in secret, held a meeting with the head of the Farm Credit Administration to tell him to "be on guard as to his financing relations of the GTA." The GTA at that time received its major funding through the Central Bank for Cooperatives, a division of the FCA. In a speech to the 1943 GTA meeting, Loriks said that no commercial bank could accommodate the GTA's credit needs, so that the FCA, through its Central Bank for Cooperatives, handled those needs.

Loriks went on to say in this speech, "Our enemies on the outside are trying to do their level best to destroy our credit relationship with the FCA. They know it is a vulnerable point of attack. We expect those attacks from our enemies. It is, however, unthinkable that any member of this board should in any manner attempt to impair our credit relationship and thereby wreck our GTA." To Loriks, the actions of the two board members, who were ousted at the 1943 meeting, were "nothing short of treason."

Also in 1943, Thatcher first suggested his National Agricultural Relations Act, an attempt to suggest ways for the farmer to have similar bargaining power to the city worker. Though never enacted, NARA was a longtime GTA concern, and at many points, both Thatcher and Loriks actively lobbied for its enactment.

After its earlier "Food for Victory" campaign during World War II, GTA after the war advanced a "Mercy Wheat Campaign," shipping in sixteen of the eighty million bushels of grain provided nationally to feed the hungry in Europe.

In 1946 and 1947, the private grain interests pursued legal action to block the GTA from buying its own members' grain. This issue was resolved by a February 14, 1947, Minnesota Supreme Court decision that held in favor of the GTA. Also in 1947, GTA moved into its new offices at Larpenteur and Snelling in St. Paul, the office location still used today by GTA's successor, Harvest States Cooperatives.

The late 1940s and early 1950s were a time of generally high farm prices and a time when GTA advocated 90 percent of parity farm prices before Congress. There was continued expansion of GTA elevators, and in 1951, a compromise was achieved on a cooperative tax law that blocked the NTEA program and satisfied the GTA directors and management.

Although the Korean War had increased demand for U.S. crops, in a few years the concern would be surpluses. By the time the Eisenhower Administration took office in early 1953, the government had on hand $1 billion worth of surplus commodities. The farmer's share of the consumer food dollar was by this time forty-six cents, the lowest since World War II. The political battle of the early 1950s was over Agriculture Secretary Ezra Taft Benson's call for a return to the "free market," with resultant lower price support levels—a position opposed by the GTA, as well as by the Farmers Union.

Although the GTA was widely perceived as favoring Democrats, it really did play both sides of the political street. Loriks wrote to and received numerous letters from such Republican figures as Representative Clifford Hope of Kansas and Senator Milton Young of North Dakota, as well as South Dakota's own Senator Karl Mundt. The two one-time political adversaries, Mundt and Loriks, had long forgotten the bitterness of the 1938 Congressional campaign and had forged a strong and long-standing working relationship on farm matters. A January 3, 1957, letter from Mundt to Loriks is indicative not only of their cooperative efforts, but also of a friendly relationship. Mundt wrote to thank Loriks for pictures taken of Mundt and his wife at a banquet in Washington and said, "I was very interested in your old campaign poster and in comparing the picture on that poster and the one of you at the Federation banquet. I see that you have not only retained a healthy head of hair, but that you are even more handsome than ever after twenty years."

Loriks seemed to be on equally close terms with North Dakota's Young, writing to Young on June 7, 1954, to say, "Farmers are recognizing you as the outstanding leader in the fight for parity in Washington. South Dakota is proud of you." In his capacity as South Dakota Farmers Union administrative assistant, Loriks invited Young to speak at the 1954 state convention.

The close working relationship that GTA had with Young did not please North Dakota Democrat Quentin Burdick, first a Congressman and later a Senator. Burdick, whose views coincided in large measure with those of the GTA, on April 12, 1956, wrote a strongly worded letter to the eleven-member GTA board, to protest a radio broadcast by Thatcher. The letter said in part:

> The speech was not objective reporting of the farm issue, but a pure political endorsement of Senator Young, done in an effective, diabolical and insidious manner. Thatcher mentioned Senators Young, Humphrey, Thye, and Mundt in the broadcast, none of whom are up for election but Senator Young.
>
> I have supported the Farmers Union and the GTA all my life, and I simply want to know where the GTA stands as an organization. The politics of the organization are carried out by you, the board members. Mr. Thatcher's announcements are in effect your announcements, since he performs administrative functions under your direction.

Thatcher, Loriks and the GTA early took an interest in the political career of South Dakota Democrat George McGovern.

While McGovern was still on the history faculty at Dakota Wesleyan University, before he resigned to devote full time to the building of the state's Democratic party, Loriks on October 31, 1952, had written to Thatcher to send "for your personal perusal a series of articles by a young man at Wesleyan University, a George S. McGovern." Thatcher wrote back on November 10 to say, "I should like to meet the young McGovern, who is apparently quite a boy. . . . Certainly from the newspaper comments, young McGovern knows his 'onions.' I shall look forward to meeting McGovern and having a good visit."

In 1955 McGovern met with Thatcher and Loriks for a strategy meeting in St. Paul at the time of the GTA convention. A McGovern letter of December 15, 1955, to Loriks mentions plans for a further strategy meeting on the 1956 political races in South Dakota, during which McGovern would run successfully for the First District Congressional seat. Loriks' letters of 1956 show that he was active in fund raising efforts for McGovern that year.

The Eisenhower-Benson farm program of the mid-1950s was one of the Soil Bank and no production controls, with a resultant drop in parity price levels to farmers. By the end of 1956, there were $6 billion in farm surpluses in the United States, a six-fold increase since the Eisenhower Administration had come into office.

Emil Loriks appears to have had a good working relationship with the sometimes difficult Thatcher during these years that Loriks was on the board and eventually vice president. Loriks did, however, over the years, receive letters from others in the GTA who were not always happy with Thatcher and his management style and policies. As far back as 1939, a fellow Farmers Union member in South Dakota had written to Loriks, on June 9, to accuse Thatcher of being on the New Deal payroll, this letter being a reflection of the long-standing unease of parts of the Farmers Union membership with the New Deal farm policies.

For his part, Thatcher appeared to like Loriks, as indicated in a January 6, 1947, letter to Loriks. "I am pleased to have this opportunity to express my complete confidence in you and your statements. I know of no one I would rather work with than you." An October 16 letter the same year, also to Loriks, thanked him and fellow South Dakota GTA board member

Members of the National Federation of Grain Cooperatives visited the Pentagon for a briefing by Department of Defense officials on March 27, 1952. Emil Loriks is second from right in the front row; M.W. Thatcher is fourth from left in front row.
Photo courtesy of South Dakota Farmers Union

August Dahme for their work: "I am doggone pleased to have you two boys with me on the GTA board. Keep on riding them, cowboy."

Ten years later, Loriks wrote to a Farmers Union associate about Thatcher: "The fact that M.W. was with us again after his recent illness did much to penetrate the smog and fog of propaganda. It seemed to vanish like mists before the noonday sun."

It was against this background of GTA expansion and political activism that Loriks served as a board member, vice president and eventually president, beginning on December 11, 1957. Throughout all the action at the GTA's high levels, Loriks never forgot the local roots of the cooperative movement, and he always took pride in being an organizer and builder of cooperatives.

Early in his GTA career, in a March 9, 1940, letter to a fellow South Dakota Farmers Union leader, Loriks had written, "We must never give up or despair in the building of the cooperative movement. It is largely a matter of education and understanding, and it may seem discouraging at times, but enough progress has been made in spots to indicate the tremendous possibilities there."

FSA Administrator

At the same time that Loriks was helping to build the grain marketing capabilities of the GTA, he also worked to support cooperatives in another way, by being first a state, and later, a regional administrator for the Farm Security Administration. In 1940 and 1941, he served as state director of the FSA in South Dakota, being based in Huron. For several months in 1942, he served as regional chief of the FSA cooperative section for an area that included North and South Dakota, Nebraska and Kansas. The regional position meant that he had to live during the week in Lincoln, Nebraska. He resigned the FSA post in December 1942 at the time he was elected national secretary-treasurer of the Farmers Union.

Loriks had been interested in working for the FSA as early as mid-1939. G.L. Moesson, manager of the Farmers Union Cooperative Brokerage of South Dakota, wrote to Loriks on June 17, 1939, to say, "Practically speaking, we are virtually drafting you into this service and trust that you will give it your most serious consideration, and that from the standpoint of the welfare of the Farmers Union, and the possibility of continued refinance plans among our cooperatives, I urge you to submit your application immediately."

The appointment obviously did not happen right away and a January 26, 1940, letter to Loriks reflected mixed feelings about his taking the job. "Emil, I am not so sure. We might need you in the Farmers Union."

By late February, things had coalesced and Loriks wrote Thatcher on February 20 about the FSA position, after just having had a call from a regional FSA official about taking the state job. Loriks wrote to Thatcher, "We certainly appreciate your interest in South Dakota and the splendid work you are doing in the interest of cooperative grain marketing. We hope to be of some assistance in expanding the grain program to our state." This was during the time when Loriks was already attending GTA board meetings on an unofficial basis.

The political nature of the FSA position is reflected in the correspondence found in the Loriks papers. For example, a letter during the fall 1940 national campaign asked Loriks to attend a rally in Aberdeen at which vice presidential nominee Henry A. Wallace would speak.

In his FSA job, Loriks also continued to write to his Congressional delegation to lobby for legislation in which he was interested. One such example was the exchange of letters between Loriks and Democratic Senator William J. Bulow, supporting Bulow's bill for extra compensation for military service personnel called into active duty. Bulow also wrote to Loriks about a postmaster appointment in South Dakota, an appointment which Loriks had not liked.

Internal policy matters and also budget cuts at the federal level were a major concern of Loriks' letters in 1941 and 1942. As war seemed certain to break out, a variety of domestic programs faced cuts. In a letter to Tom Berry on August 23, 1941, Loriks spoke of "most drastic reductions in our personnel budget which means the elimination of a large number of personnel. This of course, you realize, is the most unpleasant job that anyone can have wished upon him." He wrote Senator Bulow the same week, on August 26, to say that twenty-five to thirty persons would lose their jobs.

All the while, a main Loriks concern was with cooperatives. At one point, he conducted a survey of cooperative creameries.

Loriks also kept close tabs on South Dakota and Farm Union politics, at one point writing to Tom Berry, on September 30, 1941, to tell him about the attacks that John Skage, who had succeeded Loriks as state Farmers Union president, was making on the Republican administration of Governor Harlan J. Bushfield. The letter noted that Loriks' old foe, Ed Everson, was secretary of agriculture in the Bushfield Administration, a post he would hold until 1946. The letter to Berry ended, "The Governor now has a record to defend and I am glad somebody is analyzing the record in advance of political campaigns."

After Pearl Harbor, on December 26, 1941, Loriks wrote to regional FSA director Cal Ward, "At any rate, *victory* is the watchword now, and all our efforts will, no doubt, be directed toward achievement of that goal. Our immediate objective is to win the *war,* and in my opinion our various federal programs will survive to the extent that our efforts are integrated with some phase of national defense."

Efforts continued to convince lawmakers in Washington that the FSA was needed and supported by farmers. One poll in an Aberdeen newspaper showed 66 percent approval for the FSA and 77 percent for the Agricultural Adjustment Administration.

Sometime in early 1942, Loriks was promoted to the regional FSA office in Lincoln. Much of the mail to him in Lincoln was from persons wanting jobs with the FSA. In Lincoln, he also continued his surveys of cooperatives, at one point receiving a report from the head of the agricultural economics department at South Dakota State College about the cooperative situation in South Dakota.

An old South Dakota friend wrote a congratulatory note on May 12, 1942: "It sure gave me a real thrill of joy when I read in the papers that you had been transferred to Lincoln. I know that the Farm Security clients haven't another person who is a better friend for them. I positively know that success in great abundance is in store for you in that office."

Despite such sentiments, Loriks did not have a long career in Lincoln, quitting the position by the end of 1942 to become national Farmers Union secretary-treasurer. He did stay in close touch for several years with FSA associates and with political figures about the fate of the FSA.

Loriks' daughter has said that her father probably did not like the FSA administrative work, especially the stint in Lincoln when he had to be away from his family and from South Dakota, as much as some of the other things he did in his life. But in later years, Loriks did take pride that he had once served in this governmental capacity. He thought that perhaps he had been able to help farmers at a time when they really needed it.

John Barron, who served in the FSA under Loriks for three years, recently offered this evaluation of Loriks' career with the FSA:

> Emil was an excellent supervisor. One could always bring to him any problem and get a fair hearing. His word was as good as his bond and in all the years I worked for him, he never "let me down."
>
> How proud I am to have been a co-worker with Mr. Loriks in the Farm Security Administration,

which accomplished so much for farm people in a time of great need.

One of the reasons that I admire Mr. Loriks is that in all of his efforts, he sought no monetary or other honors for himself. He is truly one of those persons about whom it can be said, "For those causes he felt were right, he gave his damnedest."

These comments had been written in 1984, before Loriks' death. After Loriks died, Barron wrote again on February 28, 1986, to relate a story about Loriks which illustrates his concern for others and his lack of concern about himself. As he traveled on FSA business, Loriks carried in his pocket a large number of brown envelopes containing his paychecks, not having bothered to cash them. Whenever Loriks had something he wanted to remember, he got out one of those brown envelopes and recorded a note on it. Barron said, "He was too busy or forgot to go into the bank—he was much more concerned about some farm family up in Corson or Walworth County who hadn't gotten their check than he was about his own uncashed checks which he carried around the state in his coat pocket."

Farmers Union Leader

Closely related to both the GTA service and the short-lived FSA stint was Loriks' continuing involvement with and service to the Farmers Union. This was true at national and state levels. At the 1937 national Farmers Union convention, he was elected to the board, and was named secretary-treasurer in late 1942, a post from which he resigned in early 1946.

Although Loriks was no longer a state Farmers Union officer after he quit as president in 1938 to run for Congress, he continued to be very much involved, and his papers contain many letters from South Dakota Farmers Union leaders seeking his counsel. One of his responsibilities as a national board member in the early 1940s was to do organizational work in neighboring Minnesota, so this was still another reason to stay in close touch with the South Dakotans.

In the early 1950s, Loriks held the paid position of administrative assistant in the South Dakota Union, and did a variety of tasks including public relations, editing the state newspaper and being an organizer. He resigned this post in October 1956, one year before he became GTA president.

The legislative and political concerns of the Farmers Union of the 1940s and 1950s bear review. As stated in the booklet "Highlights of Agricultural Progress, Farmers Union," published in 1964, the Union, beginning in the late 1930s, had been a strong advocate of full, or at least high, parity prices for farmers. While the Roosevelt and Truman administrations were generally, but not always completely, in tune with Union positions, the Republican administration of Dwight Eisenhower was not. Parity levels came down in the Eisenhower-Benson years of the 1950s.

The Union, not surprisingly, had strong positions in favor of cooperatives and for the REA. It was a backer of the United Nations and also supported international wheat agreements. The Union was a strong backer of Public Law 480, the Agricultural Trade and Development Act of 1954, which was a start toward the Food for Peace concept that the Kennedy Administration incorporated into its program in 1961, with the naming of South Dakota's George McGovern to head that agency.

Loriks' election to the national Farmers Union board was greeted favorably by an associate from his Farm Holiday days, who wrote, in an apparent reference to the Union dissension, "It was not a surprise, but a lot of satisfaction—believe you have a board that will practice cooperation as well as preach it."

Although Loriks, as early as January 1938, had apparently been assigned by the national board to organize in Minnesota, this was open to legal challenges from the ousted Minnesota faction into 1940. Ed Everson was one of those opposing the national board's action in disbanding the one group in Minnesota. A May 28, 1938, letter from Loriks to James Patton at the national office noted that Everson had sent Loriks a registered letter to ask for evidence "incident to suspension of Minnesota and Michigan chapters."

Governor Elmer Benson of Minnesota wrote on November 23, 1938, to Loriks to offer his congratulations on the news that Loriks would be organizing Union groups in Minnesota. Although Benson wrote, "I am indeed glad that at last the way has been cleared for the building of a unified progressive farm organization in Minnesota," things were not quite that simple. The ousted faction took its case first to district court, and then to the Minnesota Supreme Court whose ruling cleared the way for Loriks and the national Union to proceed. Loriks wrote on February 4, 1940, "It seems this should clear the fog of suspicion and doubt that has hung over Minnesota, and that organization of the Farmers Union should now go forward without hestitation."

Loriks' membership on the national board was good news to his friends in the South Dakota labor movement. State Federation of Labor President Albert Maag, with whom Loriks carried on an extensive correspondence for many years, wrote on December 30, 1938, to congratulate Loriks. "I do hope you will stay on the firing line and continue to fight the battles for the masses," he wrote.

Not surprisingly, Loriks continued his heavy schedule of making speeches. On April 28, 1938, Patton, then the executive secretary of the Colorado Union as well as a national board member, wrote Loriks to say how much he had appreciated being with Loriks on the National Farmers Union Radio Hour.

When Loriks became national secretary-treasurer, one of his biggest challenges was that of the budget—reminiscent of his budget problems at the FSA. Many letters referred to that budget situation. On May 15, 1943, Loriks wrote to M.W. Thatcher that he was having to cut more than $22,000 in departmental expenditures. "We are compelled to do this to meet extra-budgetary expenditures, contingencies and emergencies not contemplated in the budget. With retrenchment in departmental expenditures must go rigid supervisions and control over all disbursements." In another letter to Thatcher on the same day, he promised to "ride herd" on expenditures, something that other Farmers Union officials apparently were not inclined to do. On December 1, 1944, Loriks wrote to a long list of Union officials to ask them to attach receipts along with their expense vouchers.

In the fall of 1944, Loriks had offered to have those in field work laid off, and he said in a September 10 letter, "I volunteered to take the lead." That fall, he apparently did not draw the paycheck to which he was entitled as national secretary-treasurer. This was a position which had paid a yearly salary to him of $4,500 in 1943.

It seems likely that some of the reasons for the national Union's continuing budget problems were related to continuing dissension in the organization. A long letter from Patton to Loriks on September 12, 1944, said, "It is unfortunate that we do have in the Farmers Union a small, but very persistent, group of people who are reactionary and, to a great degree, follow the fascist lines. If there was some way in which we could go far enough to force these people out of the organization, we would be much better off."

In an answer to Patton, Loriks wrote on October 5, "Yours is the first administration of the National Farmers Union that has given serious thought to budgeting; as a matter of fact, heretofore they never had anything really to budget."

But Loriks apparently became discouraged and disillusioned about national financial matters, and by late 1945, he had made plans to resign. In a letter that Loriks wrote to John Skage on January 23, 1946, after he had "checked out" of the secretary-treasurership, he said, "The national Farmers Union is a national poorhouse financially, and the two-bit dues just don't finance anything, so we have to beg." One year later, on January 2, 1947, Loriks again wrote to Skage to say that "sloppy national FU management of the budget was the main reason I quit."

Even though Loriks was no longer a national officer after early 1946, he did keep up his interest in the national group, and its officers continued to ask him to perform such tasks as heading the by-laws committee and making speeches on behalf of the Union. In 1947, Union president Patton asked Loriks to testify in Washington at House and Senate hearings on agricultural policy issues. Patton also periodically asked that Loriks come to national board meetings and strategy sessions. In May 1951, Loriks and Paul Opsahl, then South Dakota president, attended the International Federation of Agricultural Producers Conference in Mexico City, on behalf of the national Union. Patton wrote on June 14, 1951, to say, "I was very proud of our Farmers Union delegation. Certainly we had a group anyone could be proud of and one which presented itself in the best fashion."

During the time that Loriks held national Union office, there was apparently some sentiment to make him Extension Director at South Dakota State College. There is a copy of a telegram to that effect dated August 8, 1945, from James Patton to Loriks, saying, "Secretary Anderson advises me that he intends to recommend you as State Director of Extension." Both the state Democratic chairman and state Farmers Union president Oscar Fosheim wrote letters on Loriks' behalf, Fosheim saying in his June 12, 1946, letter to Agriculture Secretary Anderson, "Mr. Loriks subscribes to my policy of remaining on friendly terms with you and your department."

During the 1940s and 1950s, there were continuing charges, both from inside and outside the organization, that the Farmers Union was a communistic organization. Lowell K. Dyson in *Red Harvest* explained that in the 1930s there was the Popular Front period when the Communists had identified themselves with the New Deal, as did the Farmers Union and a variety of other liberal groups. There had been Communists in both the Farm Holiday and the Farmers Union.

With the advent of World War II, the common concern of the Popular Front was to defeat fascism. The Farmers Union and also the CIO supported Roosevelt's foreign and domestic policies, and the Communists during this time praised the Farmers Union for joining the progressive fight against reaction. Dyson wrote that many Farmers Union leaders, including Thatcher of the GTA, "undoubtedly approved of the Popular Front line simply because they despised war, feared fascism, and supported the New Deal."

The October 1944 issue of the *Farm Journal* contained an article about the Farmers Union called, "Communist Beachhead in Agriculture," which became the focus of many of Loriks' letters at that time. He spoke of the article and of dissent within the South Dakota Union, dissent which Loriks saw as a threat to both the state leadership of John Skage and to the national leadership. The dissent came from the old Everson faction, and Loriks in one letter used the term "fascist" to describe the dissidents. "The strategy of Fascist forces in the Union will be to stir up a lot of controversy over small, unimportant issues and get the membership into a tempest of confusion and turmoil and in that process they hope to take over. They will, of course, accuse us of Communist connections and partisan politics, probably their major issues."

The good news for Loriks in the fall of 1944 was that "the reactionaries took a beating in the election. That did my heart good," he wrote to South Dakota Farmers Union associate

Paul Erickson on November 11. "There is ten times more danger of this country going fascist than Communist. That is a false issue and they know it."

With the end of the war and the coming of the Truman Administration, the Union had its problems with both domestic and foreign policy. Union president Patton was strongly internationalist and had supported the founding of the United Nations and "without being pro-Communist," Dyson said, "he appeared to believe that a continuation of the domestic Popular Front would best guarantee liberalism at home and peace abroad." As the Cold War grew more intense by 1947, liberals became more and more divided about how to regard the Soviet Union, and those tensions were also reflected within the Union. There were anti-Communist resolutions introduced at both the 1946 and 1948 national conventions, although they did not pass. South Dakota Union members during this time did pass an anti-Communist resolution.

In April 1948, the *South Dakota Union Farmer* published a statement from President Paul Opsahl which said in part:

> Many good people in South Dakota Farmers Union have shown signs of being disturbed over the question of Communism. It has even led some of them to question the loyalty of our organization's leaders.
>
> Therefore, it seems a good time to state flatly that the officers of the South Dakota Farmers Union have always been opposed to Communism, are opposed to it, and always will be.
>
> We have no sympathy with Communism, either in theory or practice. We dislike Communists, both at home and abroad. We deplore their underground system of infiltration into liberal organizations and the inconsistency of their changing front every time the Kremlin decides to alter its policy.
>
> We implore the good people of South Dakota not to be taken in by this hysteria. Keep your feet on the ground. Adopt a positive attitude and program and maintain them boldly, fearlessly and militantly.

It was actually the Henry Wallace Progressive Party movement of 1948 that finally resulted in the Union's getting back into the Democratic party mainstream. While the Union, or at least many elements, were sympathetic to Wallace's effort, the Truman Administration took a more liberal turn, and Truman eventually appointed the liberal Charles Brannan to succeed Clinton Anderson as Secretary of Agriculture. Dyson wrote that Wallace appeared to take farmer support for granted and actually ignored farmers during the campaign.

Loriks' detachment from the Wallace movement was illustrative of that of the Farmers Union mainstream leadership. During early 1948 he apparently received many letters asking him to support Wallace and he even had a long distance call from former Minnesota Governor Benson. Loriks spelled out his misgivings in a letter to Oscar Fosheim on January 18, 1948. "Much as we might think of Henry and all the good that he has done, and the fact that we supported him with all our might at the last Demo National Convention, it would seem this is a little different deal," Loriks wrote. After listing the pros and cons of a Wallace candidacy, Loriks added, "It seems the GOP and the 'Commies' are rejoicing over the Wallace candidacy, at least so I am told." Loriks went on to tell Fosheim that the national Farmers Union newspaper had made no endorsement nor had organized labor or the North Dakota Progressive Alliance. Loriks expressed like sentiments in other letters that winter.

The South Dakota Progressive Alliance also did not endorse Wallace. Joe Robbie, who would later be best known for owning the Miami Dolphins, but at that time executive secretary of the South Dakota Alliance, wrote to Loriks on January 21, 1948, "It was the sense of all members present that it would be political suicide in South Dakota for our group to endorse Wallace, and that he is doing a disservice in 1948 to liberalism nationally by splitting the liberal vote between himself and the Democratic party."

Patton early in the year, while personally sympathetic to Wallace, deplored the candidacy, fearing it would lead to the election of a Republican president. By fall, Patton was supporting Truman. Dyson said that "the Farmers Union broke out of the Popular Front mold in 1948. The leadership rejected Wallace and overwhelmingly supported Truman."

There were bruised feelings in the Union over the 1948 political tensions, but with the appointment of Charles Brannan as Agriculture Secretary in 1949 and his presentation of the Brannan plan to preserve the family farm, unity came back to the Union.

But the Communist issue continued well into the 1950s. Union members were not in agreement about what the United States should have done about Korea. In the summer of 1950, there was considerable correspondence in the Loriks papers about a pamphlet that the American Legion had distributed in South Dakota, charging the Union with Communist leanings. President Patton wrote to Loriks on July 30 about his strategy to deal with Legion charges and he included a copy of the reply he had written to the Legion. The pamphlet had listed the Union as a "Communist front organization believed to be defunct or inactive." Patton assured the Legion that his organization was neither defunct nor inactive, and that, moreover, its charges were untrue. The pamphlet had cited a supposed report of the House Committee on Un-American Activities for its evidence about the Union; Patton had had a check made of the committee's files and could find no such report.

On August 2, Loriks wrote to thank Patton for his help in "clearing up a situation in northern South Dakota, where the Union is being smeared." He added, "This is, of course, old stuff. I wrote the Legion a couple of years ago about the matter. I hope you will be able to get a retraction from them, and also from the Hoven paper that is publicizing the contents of this old Legion pamphlet." Loriks added that he had contacted South Dakota's congressmen and also Senator Mundt to enlist their support.

Senator Mundt and Congressman Harold Lovre both wrote to Loriks on August 25 to give their support. Lovre had had information researched from the Un-American Activities Committee and had also contacted the Justice Department.

On September 7, 1950, Republican Senator Styles Bridges of New Hampshire made a speech on the Senate floor which accused both the Farmers Union and Agriculture Secretary Brannan of Communist leanings. He charged that "Communists, Communist sympathizers or Communist coddlers" had infiltrated and perhaps taken over the Union. Senators, ranging from Hubert Humphrey to Joseph McCarthy and including Mundt, North Dakota's two Republican Senators Langer and Young, and Wherry of Nebraska, rose to the Union's defense.

Mundt's endorsement could have been somewhat more ringing, in that he first said, "I do not personally know any of the present national leaders of the Farmers Union. I know nothing about whether they are or are not connected with any Communist-front organizations or any Communist groups." He went on to say, "But I can say, so far as the Farmers Union in my own state is concerned, I think I have known all the state presidents of the Farmers Union of South Dakota across the period of the last fifteen years, and they have consistently been a fine, representative group of South Dakota farmers." He ended, "Our Farmers Union members there are loyal, hard-working, patriotic and God-fearing men and women."

Congressman Lovre wrote to Union President Patton on September 21, "As far as I have been able to tell, there is no Communist influence in the South Dakota Farmers Union. It is composed of loyal American farmers. I have known state president Opsahl and state secretary Loriks for years. I can personally vouch for these gentlemen as loyal Americans sincerely interested in the problems of the family-size farmer." Lovre went on to say that he had made a public statement in a meeting at Ipswich that "there is not the slightest suspicion of Communist influence upon the leadership of the South Dakota Farmers Union."

In one instance, the Farmers Union even brought libel charges over the Communism issue. The June 15, 1951, issue of the *South Dakota Union Farmer* reported on the front page that the Farmers Union had won a $25,000 judgment against the Utah Farm Bureau for its having called the Union "Communist dominated."

A somewhat related charge surfaced the next year. On May 27, 1952, in his Mutual Radio broadcast, Fulton Lewis, Jr., said that the Brannan plan's authorship "lies in the National Farmers Union in an extreme left wing and dubious little side runt of the family of national farm organizations controlled for all practical purposes, if not by actual direction, by the CIO." Lewis apparently made a similar charge in 1953, because in April 1953, Loriks wrote to national Union secretary Tony Dechant about his efforts to refute the Lewis broadcast.

Dyson wrote that by the early 1950s, the Union in its efforts to purge itself of the Communist charges, "turned away from the past activism of the NFU and sealed a bond with the conformism of the decade."

In his sixty years of involvement with and concern about

farm policy matters, Loriks' strongest sense of identification was probably with his own South Dakota Farmers Union. Even during the years in which he was first getting involved with the GTA, Loriks still got letters urging him to take part in activities in Pierre during the legislative session. He was not above making a sarcastic comment in a January 9, 1939, letter to his successor as state president, John Skage, writing about his adversary Ed Everson's having been appointed as agriculture secretary in the administration of new Republican Governor Bushfield. He spoke of Everson's "having through his great influence as a farm leader swung the state GOP and single-handedly elected the whole GOP ticket, a bunch of candidates who were all defeated two years ago when they did not have his support. *He should now be in excellent position to shape the policies of the new administration. . . .* This is the most extraordinary opportunity he has had in a lifetime to really do something for the Farmers Union."

Loriks continued his heavy speaking schedule in 1939 speaking at the South Dakota Union convention as a representative of the national board. He enjoyed a good dispute, as he said in a letter of October 15, 1939, about that year's convention, "It was the hottest fight on any State Convention floor yet; however, the Everson payrollers were completely routed and sanity prevailed. I enjoy a good fight and ours was a peach; we won a glorious and decisive victory."

There were even times when the politically adventurous Loriks thought longingly about the farm back home. On March 9, 1940, he wrote a Union friend, "Farming seems rather peaceful at that and I have enjoyed getting back to it the last couple of years. I long since declined to run for Congress and for the State Senate here in Kingsbury and Hamlin."

There were times when the actions of the South Dakota legislature did not please him at all. On March 7, 1947, he wrote to August Dahme, who had just been chosen as the second South Dakota director to the GTA, "Well, this session of the legislature is perhaps the most ignominious failure in the history of South Dakota, and the one two years ago was bad enough! They passed all kinds of vicious anti-labor legislation and it seems that our boys went right down the line with the reactionaries voting against labor. They voted for and spent most of their time raising their own salaries and passing legislation that will mean far more taxes for everybody except

Homestake."

Loriks was also a person to whom factions of the state Union wrote to express their views, often in nearly gossipy style. In 1948, John Skage, Loriks' successor as state Union president, who had been defeated for re-election in 1944 by Oscar Fosheim by just one vote, wrote Loriks numerous letters about his dissatisfaction with state Union leadership. By this time, Paul Opsahl was president and both the Opsahl faction and the Skage side wrote Loriks letters to ask his advice and seek his support.

The Skage-Opsahl disagreement was still occurring in January 1957 when, on January 3, Loriks wrote to Skage in sympathetic terms to complain that historical papers and back issues of the *Union Farmer* had been thrown out in housecleaning at the state office. Loriks said that he had told Opsahl that he "had better look into how things are being done in his office."

In the end, Loriks, although sympathetic to Skage, did not really support Skage's plans to challenge Opsahl for the state presidency. Loriks wrote to Skage on August 17, 1957, to ask him to keep in mind the importance of his work as the manager of "the biggest FU Central Exchange Coop in South Dakota and one of the largest in the northwest and presently expanding. Would your leaving create a problem in management that might be almost insurmountable?" While praising Skage in that letter, he suggested that things might be worked out if Opsahl were to serve just one more year and Skage were not to challenge him in an election.

Loriks and Skage stayed in close touch that late summer and fall. There is a curious reference in an August 26 letter from Skage to Loriks: "I wonder if we could have a conference in Brookings quite soon. I thought about calling you but you mentioned your wires being tapped. I guess you can call me though without anyone being the wiser."

In an appeal to "what is best for the FU," an agreement was worked out for Opsahl to step down the following year. There were still bad feelings after the agreement was worked out, because Opsahl did not announce at the 1957 state convention that he would step down in 1958. Skage sent Loriks a photostatic copy of a letter that Opsahl had sent him before the convention in which he had promised to make his announcement to the convention. There were more letters back

Laying the cornerstone for the Farmers Union state office building in Huron on September 6, 1951, were, from left, president Paul Opsahl, secretary Emil Loriks, and former presidents Oscar Fosheim and John Skage.

Photo courtesy of South Dakota Farmers Union

Emil Loriks, third from left on front bench, was seen in the crowd the day of the cornerstone ceremonies.

Photo courtesy of South Dakota Farmers Union

and forth, and Skage on November 6, 1957, wrote to Loriks to say that he would really like to do something, except for the fact that Bill Thatcher "has the desire to keep things from getting too tough until after the GTA convention."

Paul Opsahl did step down in 1958, being succeeded by Harold Golseth.

There were other Farmers Union concerns in the late 1950s besides internal Union politics. One was support of the St. Lawrence Seaway, which would benefit not only South Dakota farmers, but also the GTA membership.

Loriks and Thatcher continued to exchange letters on political matters. The ever-calculating Thatcher wrote on November 25, 1953, about plans for the GTA convention that fall. "I do not think it is desirable to ask Mundt to be with us at this time," a comment that he did not explain. On October 11, 1954, Loriks wrote to Thatcher, "There is widespread sentiment against this administration; however, I am not sure that it is strong enough to upset Mundt and Lovre, especially in view of their support of 90 percent. We just can't burn all our bridges because we might have to work with them again."

During Loriks' tenure as administrative assistant in the state Union office, the organization finally determined its permanent headquarters—in Huron—and on May 10, 1952, dedicated its new office building. This ended years of moving the office from city to city. The price tag for the new building was modest by today's standards—$130,000, according to the April 1954 *GTA Digest.*

On August 11, 1956, Loriks notified directors of the South Dakota Union and the press of his decision to leave the state staff in October. The press release he issued noted his re-election to a three-year term as a GTA board member and his being GTA vice president. He said that he "planned to devote more time to personal affairs and farming interests and also that he would devote more time to coop promotion and development than he had been able to do in recent years."

It seems likely that Loriks was looking ahead to becoming GTA president and wanted an interval for personal consolidation.

After leaving the state Union office, he continued to stay in touch with state Union leaders, writing to Ben Radcliffe on January 3, 1957, about possible strategy to advocate an increase in the ore tax. By January 17, he was writing from the

One of the inspiring moments of the 1952 South Dakota
Farmers Union convention at the Mitchell Corn Palace was
the group singing. Song leader Julian Holter of Canton
brought the crowd to its feet for community singing. In Emil
Loriks' words, "It was a rhythmic symphony of human voices
from the grassroots singing songs of the soil." President Paul
Opsahl is at the left, while Emil Loriks is at the far right next
to vice president Harold Golseth, who would later succeed Opsahl in the presidency.

Photo courtesy of South Dakota Farmers Union

St. Charles Hotel in Pierre, "It seems Pierre is swarming with
Homestake lobbyists now." In this same legislative session,
Loriks lobbied for salary increases for South Dakota judges,
and at least two Supreme Court justices and one circuit judge
wrote to thank him and the Union for their support.

A February 24, 1948, letter to a Farmers Union associate
summed up his feeling on being a progressive in a conservative
state. "The reactionaries have a tremendous advantage over
us progressives, in that they have but one objective they could
all agree on, namely to preserve the status quo—in other
words, *do nothing*. We progressives often have too many
divergent routes for accomplishing things and consequently
there is division in our own ranks."

All this service to the Grain Terminal Association, the Farm
Security Administration and the Farmers Union at national
and state levels had a common thread—that of promotion and
development of cooperatives. In his final GTA speech in 1967,
Loriks looked back at the 1930s, 1940s and 1950s and said,
"The field was ripe for building cooperatives, and this became

my mission. Our resources were slim. Those early cooperatives were built by the determination of farm families."

It seems fitting that one of the last honors Loriks received the fall before he died in 1985 was to be one of the first two persons named as charter members of the new South Dakota Coop Hall of Fame. The story in the November *East River Guardian* called him "One of the giants of the cooperative movement." This award particularly pleased Loriks.

A November 1964 *GTA Digest* article entitled "The Colorful Career of Emil Loriks" described him as "quiet, but energetic" and "as active and aggressive today as he was when he helped found the Farmers Holiday Association in 1932."

Loriks' daughter, Ruth Ann, in a July 1982 interview, described her father's "boundless energy" and how he seemed to require less sleep than most other people. It has to have been that "boundless energy" that fueled his passage through the years from 1939 to 1957 and prepared him to take on the job of the GTA presidency at the end of 1957.

Emil Loriks as GTA president.
Photo courtesy of Madison *Daily Leader*

CHAPTER VI

GTA President, 1957-1967

Emil Loriks became president of the Farmers Union Grain Terminal Association on December 11, 1957. As he observed ten years later in his final annual report, his presidency was an era of "diversification and expansion in the processing of grain." The emphasis in the early GTA years had been on marketing, while the Loriks years were to see the GTA "transformed from a grain commission and storage operation into an integrated marketing and processing enterprise." Another important thrust for GTA during the late 1950s and the 1960s was legislation. Given the legislative background and acumen of both Loriks and GTA manager Thatcher, it is not surprising that legislation was very important, although this emphasis may have been somewhat less than it had in the early 1950s.

Loriks received many letters of congratulation on becoming GTA president. Among the many politicians who wrote was Senator William Langer of North Dakota. "I hope you will let me hear from you if you have any suggestions on new legislation or any other matter that you feel I should know about," Langer said.

An indication of Loriks' priorities and concerns can be found in the speeches he delivered at the GTA annual conventions. On December 12, 1960, he spoke of America's farm surpluses. "This abundance can be the shield and armor of our America, and the free world, if we only learn to use it as food for peace." He continued, "the real truth, which many city people fail to understand is that food prices have gone up in the face of falling farm prices." His hopes for the GTA were that "It must become the dominant voice of agriculture in the markets and in Washington, and it must join the people of other nations in the simple but significant task of developing a cooperative program of peace through abundance."

It will be helpful to examine the Loriks presidency of the GTA both in terms of organizational matters and GTA growth, and also in terms of its political and agricultural policy stance.

In the first four years of his tenure, there were several key expansions. One was the purchase of the McCabe Elevator Company with its fifty-seven elevators and feed mills. The GTA also built modern feed plants in Edgely, N.D., and Ellis, S.D., and continued to increase the capacity of its elevators throughout the system. Another key purchase was that of forty-two elevators and related facilities in southern Minnesota from the Archer-Daniels Midland (ADM) Company.

Also in the first four years of the Loriks presidency, GTA purchased the Honeymead Products Company of Mankato, Minnesota—the largest soybean processing plant in the nation. In 1961, just a year after the ADM and Honeymead purchases, the GTA acquired the Minnesota Linseed Oil Company, with its modern flax crushing and processing plant in Minneapolis.

In 1965, GTA acquired the Froedtert Malt Corporation of Milwaukee and the next year it started a research farm near its Ellis plant. In 1967, GTA handled 175 million bushels of grain and realized savings of $4.2 million—major growth since its somewhat humble beginnings in 1938.

In speaking of all this expansion in his 1961 annual report, Loriks said, "every move we make is designed to enable us to give better service to farmers. How we are able to adapt integration to benefit the farmer may well determine whether many of us stay on the farm."

All of this expansion did not occur without some stress within the organization, a situation which Loriks addressed in his 1963 GTA convention address. "Economists warn us that to survive in any economy of giant organization we must take over more of the processing steps for the commodities we market," he asserted. "This vertical integration enables farmers to retain control of their products and benefit from the greater returns in the processing of commodities."

A report written by Roy Hendrickson of Washington, D.C., sometime during Loriks' tenure as president, provides clues about his presidential style. Hendrickson, executive secretary of the National Federation of Grain Cooperatives said, "Now, Emil Loriks, president of the GTA, turns the chairmanship of the meeting over to the vice president. He is at home on the rostrum. He makes a short, moving speech. The policy being

M.W. Thatcher, GTA founder and its general manager until May 1968.

Photo courtesy of South Dakota Farmers Union

James G. Patton, national Farmers Union president, 1940-1966.

Photo courtesy of South Dakota Farmers Union

followed, he explains, is an effort to help the young man as well as the older supporters of GTA. It represents a 'bridge between generations of GTA owners. The delegates vote, somewhat more overwhelmingly than before, for the Loriks position."

The diplomatic and persuasive skills alluded to by Hendrickson are also illustrated in the many letters back and forth between Loriks and General Manager Thatcher, and also between Loriks and other GTA board members. There were apparently difficulties in having everyone get along. It was also apparently the pattern for at least some of the board members to meet in advance of the meetings to discuss their strategy.

There always seemed to be somewhat of an undercurrent between Thatcher and other board members, with Loriks the one who was in touch with all parties. An August 7, 1957, letter to Loriks from a GTA executive assistant said that it was necessary for the GTA board to provide work space in Thatcher's home for extra hours of work. The details of financing were still pending, "with the reliance that an agreement can be reached later with GTA to pay Mr. Thatcher a fair rental to cover the investment and the repairment of his house."

Throughout his presidency, Loriks always addressed the general manager as "Dear Mr. Thatcher." Early in his term, there were letters from Loriks to Thatcher that set a generally positive tone. On September 5, 1958, Loriks wrote, "Just a word to tell you how much I appreciate being called in yesterday. It gave me the biggest lift since I became president of the GTA board—the administrative decision you have made—all in line with GTA's march of progress in 1958." Loriks ended the letter, "Last December I was a bit hesitant about taking on the presidency; however, I can tell you now I am happy to serve in that capacity and to be in position to cooperate with you in the great work you are doing—building GTA."

There were other mutual admiration letters between Loriks and Thatcher. On February 28, 1958, Thatcher had written to thank Loriks for his "great skill in presenting this matter and also the usual tact, which you have, helped immensely; I am very grateful to you." For his part, Loriks was just as glowing in a June 27, 1958, letter to Thatcher, following a board meeting. "Wanted to convey to you that I am very much pleased with the outcome. Your powerful presence penetrated the smog of propaganda and caused it to vanish like mists before the noonday sun."

Thatcher was, to be sure, a commanding personality. In his chapter on Thatcher for the book *Great American Cooperators,* GTA research director Robert Handschin wrote, "His personal warmth to those he served or worked with also characterized his platform speaking, at which he became a master. Friend of presidents, senators and congressman, he also could make each farmer and his wife in a large audience feel his personal concern for them, or could be thoughtful about small details in the lives of those he met."

For all these comments, it sometimes took diplomatic skills on Loriks' part to try to settle misunderstandings and disputes between Thatcher and other GTA personnel. On January 12, 1958, Loriks wrote to a Montana Farmers Union official who had written to Loriks to criticize Thatcher for having cut National Farmers Union President James Patton short in a speech at the GTA convention. "Relative to the curtailment of Mr. Patton's speaking time at our GTA banquet, I am sure that it was due to unavoidable circumstances, the time schedule for the Humphrey broadcast which could not be changed. I am sure Jim understood this and I will say, that in my opinion, he rose mightily to the occasion." Loriks went on to say, "He did what few can, deliver a speech in three or four minutes, and it was one that will be long remembered—yes, perhaps better than if he had talked an hour."

Fellow GTA board members turned to Loriks with their complaints and concerns. On January 27, 1969, a Minnesota GTA board member wrote Loriks about his recent trip to GTA headquarters in St. Paul: "I didn't like what I saw and heard," referring to dissension between Paul Thatcher, M.W. Thatcher's son who was working in an administrative job, and others in the organization. In the letter, Paul Thatcher was said to be at "the bottom" of "considerable dissension" in the building.

The Paul Thatcher situation, along with other charges of nepotism in the Thatcher family, was one of the first challenges for Loriks in his presidency. A group in North Dakota in the summer of 1958 sent letters to GTA board members about "nepotism as now practiced in the GTA," citing Paul Thatcher and also two other Thatcher sons, Drs. Robert and John, who had chiropractic offices in GTA headquarters.

During the summer of 1958, Loriks met with some of the protesting North Dakotans, one of whom wrote on July 29 to Loriks, "Your consideration of our pleas, your respect for both sides of the issues appealed, and your general conduct of the meeting of the cooperative was a truly democratic way of doing business." Loriks and the rest of the GTA board signed a statement to the North Dakotans that said, "The GTA Board of Directors will give serious consideration to matters presented by your delegation specifically relating to policy. Major changes in top administrative personnel will be subject to Board review and approval." Accompanying this July 28 statement was a terse statement signed by manager Thatcher, "I enthusiastically support the above statement of the GTA Board of Directors."

Despite Thatcher's lengthy defense of his son Paul and his hope on September 29 that "the episode is ended," the younger Thatcher did submit his resignation in an emotional letter to the board.

At the same time the dissension over Paul Thatcher was occurring, there were also the negotiations for the McCabe Elevator Company, with the signing of the contract between M.W. Thatcher and Ben McCabe, who were, in the words of the St. Paul *Pioneer Press*, "two of the most colorful titans of the grain business," on September 13. The Loriks letters indicate that while Loriks was kept well informed about the McCabe negotiations, the real work was done by Thatcher. For his part, Loriks made a special trip to St. Paul a few days later to attend a welcome dinner at GTA headquarters for the McCabe employees. Ben McCabe, in a September 23 memo to his employees, referred to a "sincere and friendly welcome" from GTA president Loriks.

In a September 21 story, the St. Paul *Pioneer Press* said that "in terms of elevator capacity, the GTA will probably become the largest grain merchandiser in the nation on October 1."

There were three major acquisitions—within a period of thirteen months—in 1960 and 1961. There was the purchase of Honeymead Products of Mankato to process both flaxseed and soy beans, and there was also the purchase of the Archer-Daniels Midland Commander Elevator Division, both in 1960. The GTA purchase of Minnesota Linseed Oil Company followed.

To be sure, all this expansion was not effected without at

least some dissent within the GTA. On July 22, 1960, a North Dakota group, which included some of the same persons who had protested about Paul Thatcher's position, wrote all GTA board members to tell them not to take any action to purchase soybean storage and processing facilities until GTA members could discuss the project at the next annual meeting in the late fall.

The Honeymead acquisition brought the Andreas brothers into GTA decision making. A Minneapolis *Morning Tribune* story of August 3, 1960, written at the time the deal was pending, said that Dwayne O. Andreas would continue as chairman of Honeymead and that Lowell would continue as president. Dwayne, in fact, would become an executive vice president of GTA, and both brothers came to play roles as speakers at subsequent GTA annual meetings.

Right after the Honeymead acquisition, Loriks, in a January 16, 1961, letter to Thatcher, welcomed the addition of Dwayne Andreas. "I believe that Mr. Andreas is everything you said he is. His coming into our organization at this time was providential."

The GTA paid $1.5 million for the ADM line of elevators, which were, in the main, located in southwestern Minnesota. The Honeymead purchase, which had occurred just one week before the ADM, had cost GTA $6 million. Thatcher defended the two acquisitions in an August 10 memo to board members, saying that without the expansion, the whole future of grain coops "is endangered in many ways," including, he said, "a tendency to turn inward to internal controversy as part of our members get into serious difficulty and part are still getting along."

Old Farmers Union friend John Skage, for one, applauded GTA and the things that it was doing during the Loriks presidency. He wrote in January 1961 to say, "No wonder the GTA draws the largest number of farmers into its annual meetings. Here is an organization that is getting things done. *How proud I am to be a part of this show.*"

Fellow GTA board member Ervin Schumacher of North Dakota also liked Loriks' work. He wrote on November 26, 1964, right at the end of Loriks' seventh year as GTA president, to say, "Congrats to you on your re-election and choice as president of the GTA board. It is not an exaggeration, when I say, many people remarked to me on how well they like your chairing our meetings and none had a complaint." Schumacher and Loriks in May and June of 1964 had traveled to Europe to study cooperatives, with their travels taking them to Sweden, where they met with the Swedish prime minister, a visit arranged by Minnesota Senator Hubert Humphrey, and also to Denmark, Spain, Portugal, Italy, West Germany and Finland. The August-September 1964 *GTA Digest* reported that Loriks was especially impressed by the cooperatives in Sweden, the country of his father's birth.

In March 1964, Loriks also gave a speech on behalf of GTA to the national Farmers Union convention. Dwayne Andreas had originally been asked to give the speech, but asked Loriks to speak in his place because he, Andreas, did not feel he could refrain from chastising the United States Department of Agriculture. Apparently, Andreas felt that Loriks could handle the situation tactfully.

Loriks used this speech to reaffirm the Farmers Union triangle of cooperation, legislation, and education and also to call for a "more modern financing for our coops in this day of larger farm investment and credit needs."

In 1965, there was another major expansion in the form of the purchase of the Froedtert Malt Company of Milwaukee and a supplier affiliate. The August 19, 1965, Minneapolis *Morning Tribune* said that the deal was for cash, for "several million dollars." This time, even Loriks expressed a few doubts about such a large deal. He wrote to Schumacher on August 11, indicating that he and Schumacher both wanted to go over the contracts before the next board meeting. "You will recall it took us several years to learn what was in the fine print of the Honeymead deal," Loriks wrote.

Questions on the part of Loriks and other board members about the Honeymead arrangements had been raised to GTA management starting in the fall of 1964. One of the reasons for the questions was that the GTA at that time was starting to use private banks for some of its financing, having used the Bank for Coops previously. Some of the money was, in fact, coming from the Andreas group, which counted banking among its many interests. Loriks and other board members had had trouble getting management to spell out the arrangements whereby the Andreas group was drawing upward of $1 million on a ten-year program of acquisition. Loriks wrote to a fellow board member on January 14, 1965, "Am sure that not one single director had this picture until now. It should of course have been spelled out in the beginning."

On the same day that Loriks wrote to the board member, he wrote to Thatcher to explain why he had persisted in getting this arrangement all spelled out. "My chief reason for pursuing this matter persistently was not entirely my own, but at the request of several members of the GTA board after the adjournment of our November meeting."

At the time of the Froedtert negotiations, on June 6, 1965, Loriks wrote to another board member to say, "I, for one, would not want to commit GTA to a $13 to $14 million deal over 40 years. They did not bring it up in Board meeting either."

Loriks' concerns continued that summer, as he said in a letter to Schumacher on July 20, indicating that Dwayne Andreas wanted a lease arrangement. "My old fashioned belief still clings to the idea that ownership is preferable and having depreciation working for us instead of the other fellow. I also favor financing by the Bank for Coops, for they will stay with us in stormy weather! I do not have that sort of confidence in other creditors."

Loriks concluded the letter to Schumacher by saying, "These are just a few things I have in mind we should visit about and study carefully before being stampeded into another deal where the Andreas group participate in the earnings without any investment or risk on their part."

There was a lengthy postscript:

> I asked MW a couple of months ago if he thought the Andreases were as interested in building GTA as they are in building their own financial empire. They're doing well in the latter pursuit while working for us??? He put his head in his hands and replied, "I don't know."
>
> Somehow we cannot avoid this conflict of interest and therefore it behooves this Board of Directors representing 150,000 or more patrons to be alert and protect their interests at all times.

When the Froedtert deal was closed and announced to the press on August 19, Loriks still had questions. He wrote two fellow board members that he had received a note to sign for $15.5 million for the Bank for Cooperatives without an explanation of what it was for from GTA management. He had had to call Thatcher and at least one other management person to find out. "This is the first time we've been called upon to sign a note for GTA, I believe," Loriks wrote. On August 18, he had commented to Schumacher about "Andreas ingenuity" and said, "This time we should be vigilant, wide-awake and alert."

It seems likely that Loriks and the other GTA board members were able to influence the Froedtert negotiations so that it was a purchase rather than a lease and so that the Bank for Cooperatives was used for financing, rather than private banks. This was also probably the crucial interval during which board members started laying plans to get the Andreas brothers out of the GTA.

In the last two years of the Loriks GTA presidency, the main concern would be the difficult and long negotiations to get the Andreas brothers severed from the GTA and to arrange a financial settlement. Dwayne Andreas' resignation from his GTA position occurred in January 1966, and in mid-February, Andreas was named to the board of directors and executive committee of ADM. He had been a GTA vice president for nearly five years. According to a Minneapolis *Morning Tribune* article of February 20, 1965, Andreas had seen no conflict in the GTA-Honeymead arrangement, "despite widespread opinion that the cooperative movement and the free enterprise system are somehow incompatible."

The *Tribune* article went on to credit Andreas with pushing the GTA into the profitable processing of flax, malting barley and feeds, in addition to soybeans. "The 1965 GTA annual report showed that these, and not the grain business, were the only part of the operation that made any money." Andreas was also a political friend of both Thomas Dewey and Senator Hubert Humphrey, to whose vice presidential campaign he gave $10,000 in 1964.

Closely related to the Andreas matters were continuing concerns over the operations of Froedtert, and the ability of manager Thatcher to reach Froedtert president Dudley Seay on a regular basis.

In a January 25, 1966, letter to a GTA board member, Loriks communicated his apprehensions about both matters. "Have communicated my apprehensions to MW with the admonition to be alert. My conclusion is that we must keep close watch on this situation, and if disloyalty develops, be prepared to act!"

There was continuing correspondence between Loriks and other GTA board members and with Thatcher all through 1966 about attempts to reach a financial settlement with the Andreas brothers. On January 13, 1967, Loriks said in a letter to Ervin Schumacher that "Interoceanic [the Andreas family investment company] is making further demands. Are they like Shylock of old, demanding a further 'pound of flesh?' And are we dealing with people to whom money means nothing? The Honeymead deal has been a gold mine for them, and our proposed settlement seemed to be most generous." On the same day, Thatcher wrote Loriks to say, "I have had 15 months of 'hell.' It looks as though we are near the end of the grind with the two young men in Minneapolis."

On February 3, 1967, the Minneapolis *Tribune* reported that Lowell Andreas, then manager of the GTA Honeymead processing plant in Mankato, would soon be named the ADM executive vice president.

A final financial settlement was close. Loriks wrote Thatcher on February 4, "Your strategy in the matter of concluding settlement of the Andreas contract seems to be working out OK. In my opinion, you have handled this just right." Referring again to the Andreas brothers, Loriks said, "They can buy their way into control of ADM, which no doubt is preferable to being with GTA, so a clean separation at this point is desirable for all concerned."

Also on February 4, Loriks wrote Schumacher that the Andreas brothers "will put ADM on wheels and control it." Loriks also stressed the need for use of GTA's legal counsel in the negotiations.

In the same letter, Loriks talked about Thatcher's impending retirement as GTA general manager:

> It would seem that MW can wind up his illustrious career by actively promoting the development of the coop export program, being president of the Federation of Grain Cooperatives. It will be done regardless, and he can logically assume leadership. The National Agricultural Relations Act, too, and the timing is right for this to complement the effort in cooperative marketing in the field of foreign exports. The timing for this is NOW!"

On February 20, Loriks wrote to Jewell Haaland, GTA board member from Minnesota, to say that negotiations with the Andreas brothers "have been concluded on the basis we agreed upon, so hopefully this closes a most unusual chapter in GTA." The GTA board was scheduled to get a complete report when it met in Oklahoma City in March at the time of the National Farmers Union convention.

One other internal organizational matter took Loriks' attention at the end of his presidency—that of effecting the retirement of M.W. Thatcher, by then in his eighties. In a May 1966 letter, Loriks, referring to Thatcher, had spoken of a "management transition." A fellow board member wrote to Loriks on March 6, 1967, "It's about time we let Bill know who is running the show," in reference to a personnel matter that the board members wanted handled one way, and Thatcher another.

Also by the spring of 1967, board members in their letters to Loriks were talking about implementing a retirement-at-age-seventy policy, which would, of course, mean Thatcher's retirement, but would also mean in the end that Loriks would have to give up the presidency, as he turned seventy-two that summer. In a March 21 letter to Loriks, Schumacher said, "If we had a seventy-year retirement to start with, we could have an 'out.' " He continued, "I can't see any good reason why we can't take a seventy-year program on the line. This will do more for our relations in the country than any one other thing we are now doing."

The retirement age policy was implemented, resulting in Loriks' stepping down in December 1967 and in Thatcher's finally retiring the following May, right after his eighty-fifth birthday.

The other major theme, besides expansion, of the Loriks presidency was the continuing effort to influence farm policy. It was a Thatcher byword that "Farm Prices are Made in Washington," and both Thatcher and Loriks epitomized the practice of that slogan.

The early years of Loriks' GTA presidency coincided with the final years of the Eisenhower Administration. Parity levels were lower than they had been under earlier Democratic administrations and there would be $7.3 billion in farm surpluses by the time Eisenhower left office in early 1961. During the Eisenhower tenure, the long-awaited and much anticipated St. Lawrence Seaway was opened, making GTA Lake Superior facilities accessible to ocean shipping. Another crucial happening during the Eisenhower years was that Thatcher enlisted the aid of Vice President Nixon to head an Internal Revenue Service threat in regard to taxing local coops, and from that point on, the Republican Nixon and the nominally Democratic GTA were friends.

In the presidential candidacy of Democrat John F. Kennedy in 1960, the GTA placed great hope. During the campaign, Kennedy visited GTA offices in St. Paul, and said, "Agriculture is the number one domestic issue." He promised to work to raise farm income to full parity levels as soon as it was feasible to do so. Key farm states voted for Kennedy that fall in a very close election, and in December, Kennedy wired the GTA annual convention that "farm income can and must be improved."

As Kennedy started his term, parity ratios were at 80 percent, and dollar income for farmers was down 24 percent over the preceding eight years. The farmer's share of the retail food dollar stood at 39 cents, and the number of farms was 3.8 million, down from 5 million eight years before.

During the Kennedy Administration, in 1962, there was a final settlement on the issue of taxation of cooperative savings, with a single tax due by patron and the coop required to pay at least 20 percent cash back each year. Despite Administration efforts, farm surpluses continued to mount, especially with the record corn and soybean crops of 1963.

One of many Farmers Union trips to Washington, D.C., to lobby for farm legislation. Emil Loriks (wearing dark hat and at base of stairs) was ready to board for a 1965 "Fly-In."

Emil Loriks visits at a banquet with his one-time political rival Senator Karl Mundt, with whom he forged a close working relationship on farm matters, and with Mary Mundt.
Photo courtesy of Ruth Ann Carlson

The GTA thought that in Orville Freeman, agriculture secretary in the Kennedy and Johnson administrations, and a former Minnesota DFL governor, it would have a real friend. But all did not turn out as happily as anticipated. At several points, GTA was sharply critical of Freeman policies and farm decisions, so GTA continued its political stance of "playing both sides of the street." GTA not only allied itself with such liberal Democratic farm state senators as Hubert Humphrey, but also with such Republican senators as Mundt, Young and Langer. There are also found in the Loriks papers copies of letters to southern Democrats who were regarded as favorable to GTA farm policy wishes.

Typical of the letters to Humphrey was a Loriks note to him on December 27, 1957, to thank him for his speech at the GTA annual meeting. Humphrey wrote back, "Dear Emil,—Thanks so much for that wonderful letter. You have always been a wonderful friend. Sincerely, Hubert H."

Both Loriks and Thatcher had an extensive correspondence with South Dakota lawmaker Mundt, especially about legislation favorable to cooperatives and also about GTA's efforts to prevent shipments of oats out of South Dakota by the Commodity Credit Corporation (CCC). On April 23, 1959, Mundt wrote Thatcher to confirm that he had set up a luncheon with Vice President Nixon in Washington to include Thatcher and various Congressional leaders.

GTA needed to do a delicate balancing act in South Dakota as it was favorably inclined to both Republican Mundt and Democrat George McGovern. A November 5, 1959, Thatcher memo to the GTA board said in part:

> As you know, I am committed to advising the people of South Dakota the full truth about Senator Mundt's activities in helping us with the great fight for cooperatives in the field of taxation. . . . There is no other commitment to him.
>
> Since our good friend, George McGovern, is going to run for the Senate in 1960, I hope you will agree with me that we should not put Mundt on the program at the stockholders' banquet, where he would have access to the whole northwest through the radio outlet. I am especially bothered about it since McGovern is going to run against him.

Not all South Dakota Farmers Union personnel were happy with Thatcher's decision to be friendly with Mundt. Skage had written to Loriks on May 22, 1958, "I just read another of Senator Karl Mundt's newsletters. It is most nauseating." The letter went on to criticize Mundt for his colorful anti-communism. "With farmers going broke at a tremendous rate, a U.S. Senator with time on his hands could be most helpful in our hour of need, if he would only apply himself to the real problems at hand. I think the best way to fight Communism is to destroy the conditions that breed Communists."

During his first year as agriculture secretary, Orville Freeman was invited to address the GTA annual meeting in December 1961. In his letter of invitation, Thatcher practically told Freeman what to say. On December 4, he wrote, "I urge you to give special attention to the place of cooperatives on the farm front. I know how strongly you feel in support of them, but I would be disappointed if you didn't make some pretty flat statements to this great bunch of cooperators."

Relations with Freeman were soon to chill. The GTA felt

that the Freeman 1962 farm bill did not "put cooperatives in their proper place to help farmers improve their income." The GTA, in fact, criticized the National Farmers Union for its more enthusiastic support of the bill.

A March 7, 1962, Thatcher letter to Farmers Union presidents in Minnesota, Montana, North Dakota and South Dakota—the GTA area— criticized the USDA for its growth in marketing. "Certainly, the continuous takeover by the government of the warehousing and marketing normally done by farmers' cooperatives will put the farmers in a weaker position when they seek to deal with buyers in the marketplace."

Relations with Freeman were still icy in early 1963. A letter from Thatcher's secretary (and sister-in-law), Veronica Boesel, to Loriks on March 1 described a meeting that Thatcher had had in Washington with Freeman and Humphrey:

> The real problem lies with the Secretary of Agriculture whose bureaucrats have led him to the precipice of devastation of the whole marketing system as it pertains to grain and oil needs. Mr. Thatcher will go over this in detail with the board in April. For the time being, he has talked the Secretary out of this vicious program.

Despite irritations with Freeman, the GTA lines of communication were still kept open to the Kennedy Administration. On April 1, 1963, the President wrote Thatcher to commend him on his leadership as president of the National Federation of Grain Cooperatives.

During the Kennedy Administration, Loriks and Thatcher both wrote letters to and received letters from such diverse politicians as Mundt, Young, McGovern and Quentin Burdick (North Dakota).

The Kennedy Administration became the Johnson Administration with the tragic assassination of Kennedy on November 22, 1963. Freeman continued as agriculture secretary, and about Freeman, Loriks wrote on January 25, 1964, in a letter to GTA headquarters, "Freeman's attitude, it seems to me, borders on defiance against practically all grain marketing agencies in the USA. This is difficult to understand. I trust that it was not motivated by any personal feelings against us on his part, or inspired by any organization hostile to GTA."

On February 19, Thatcher wrote to Loriks from his winter address in Florida that he had met with Senator Humphrey to tell him what GTA thought of the current administration. (Humphrey was visiting Dwayne Andreas in Miami.) Thatcher wrote to Loriks about his meeting with Humphrey, "I am sure he doesn't want to see me for a month. I told him what I thought of this administration; that as of the present time, I wouldn't vote to return it to office; and that so far as agriculture is concerned, Eisenhower and Benson were 'guardian angels' compared to this show." Thatcher continued, "I think we have everything to gain and nothing to lose by blasting Freeman's administration in every way we can with our paper and our radio programs, using due care to realize that the farmers do not know the facts." Thatcher also criticized the National Farmers Union and its president, James Patton, for not being militant enough on farm matters.

On February 21, Loriks wrote to thank Thatcher for his "very frank appraisal of the situation we face in Washington." He went on, "There was strong language in your letter, but as Humphrey once said when visiting us at GTA—'You have to kick your friends on the shins once in a while lest they take us for granted.'" Loriks did warn Thatcher about getting too far afield from the rest of the Farmers Union on his stands—"There is always the danger of getting too far ahead and over the hill with the lantern."

The Loriks letter also indicated that Humphrey, in the wake of his visit with Thatcher, was starting to be helpful on the wheat legislation that GTA wanted.

On February 24, Loriks wrote to Thatcher again, "When Freeman took over USDA, we felt that we had a friend at the helm, one whose administration of USDA would strengthen, not weaken, coops in the field of marketing. For more than two years we seem to have had a running fight against policies proposed that would be injurious to farmers and their coops, some of which you were able to head off, but of late, there seems to be a dogged determination to shove such policies down our throat!"

Relations with Republicans continued to be favorable. Young wrote Loriks on May 13, 1964, to thank GTA for including one of his Senate speeches in the *GTA Digest*. "It was pretty nice of you folks, Emil, to carry my entire Senate speech."

Humphrey apparently got back in GTA's good graces, as Humphrey, by this time the Democratic vice presidential candidate, addressed the 1964 GTA convention in the fall. Thatcher sent him a $2,500 honorarium on January 8, 1965. Thatcher had warm words for both Hubert and Muriel Humphrey in his letter.

On February 23, 1965, Humphrey wrote to "Dear Ruth and Emil," to thank them for their letter of congratulations on his becoming vice president and to say, "Be assured, I am in continued close touch with USDA and will do all that I can to assure an equitable U.S. farm policy." Humphrey also thanked Loriks for his work as chairman of Rural Citizens for Johnson and Humphrey.

There continued to be ups and downs with the Johnson Administration, and Loriks continued to write both Republican and Democratic senators to get their help for farm legislation. On May 12, 1965, Loriks wrote Thatcher to ask that GTA continue to work through both parties for bipartisan support of GTA efforts. "Bipartisan protests are much more effective than if it comes only from GOP members." Two days later, Loriks wrote to a GTA official, "It is strange that we have to fight a rearguard action when our friends are in."

Nixon, Mundt, Thatcher and Loriks all appeared at a Sioux Falls fund-raising dinner, and on July 5, Mundt wrote Thatcher to thank him for pictures of the event and to offer to have Nixon autograph pictures for him.

Democrat George McGovern was also frustrated with Freeman. He wrote to Thatcher on July 8 to offer this analysis: "I do not know anyone who can persuade Orville Freeman over to a new attack, nor am I sure that winning him over would change the Administration's position. Farm policy is now being made at the White House level as a byproduct of budget policy by men without understanding of the grassroots consequences involved. They have been able to get the support of a busy president on the plea of budget necessity."

In a letter of September 22 to Freeman, Thatcher spoke more softly than he had earlier, saying that their differences were not personal, and thanking him "for your success in putting through a good farm bill. It is the best we have had in a long time, and I will be enthusiastic in my support of it, as always."

Thatcher's troubles with Freeman and his sometimes unhappiness with the National Farmers Union converged in a speech he gave at the National Union convention in March 1967. Loriks urged Thatcher to accept President Tony Dechant's invitation to speak, saying that Dechant, "realizes we must have a united front. He [Dechant] is the modest, unassuming kind as I have known him over the past many years and he does not seek any personal glory out of any success we may achieve working together."

Freeman and Thatcher were both convention speakers, Thatcher with some apparent lack of moderation. Thatcher wrote to Freeman on April 21 to apologize for "a serious mistake on my part. I could have made my points in my Oklahoma speech with a better choice of words and with less anger, but what made matters worse was that those statements were picked up and put in our broadcast, which goes into so many hands and is heard by so many people." He continued, "Not only do I take full responsibility for everything that has been said and broadcast, but I do want to say to you that it was poorly handled. I could have done the job with the care and grace that you were entitled to and therefore, I offer my apology for implying your lack of understanding or sincerity regarding cooperatives in any respect."

Loriks was very upset by the Thatcher National Farmers Union speech. Writing to a GTA board member on March 19, four days after the speech, Loriks referred to President Dechant's having read a telegram at the banquet from Thatcher apologizing for a statement Thatcher had made in his speech, charging that Robert Kennedy had voted *against* the 1965 Farm Act. "You probably remember this, and the fact is that Kennedy voted *for* the 1965 Farm Act. Can't understand how or why this could happen since he has access to information on such matters. At any rate, it was a bit embarrassing!" Loriks, in the letter, also wondered whether Thatcher might have been "a little milder" in his treatment of Freeman in that speech.

The GTA continued to like Nixon, that unlikely friend of GTA. Veronica Boesel explained in a letter to Loriks on May 5, 1967, that Nixon, as vice president, had gotten the IRS commissioner to reverse a ruling under which "as many as half of the cooperatives in the southwest and a great many in our area would have been bankrupted. . . . Regardless of any other feelings we may have about Mr. Nixon, I think we must all be grateful to him for this activity which saved so many cooperatives."

Also in March 1967, Loriks wrote to thank Vice President Humphrey for sending him a pair of cuff links. "Thank you again for your ever thoughtful consideration of old friends, even from little and remote corners like South Dakota, and in a time of multiple world crises when you are so deeply involved in the problems of the entire world."

Loriks continued to work behind the scenes for George McGovern, who would face a re-election campaign for his Senate seat in 1968. In early 1967, Loriks even asked Dwayne Andreas to make a contribution to the McGovern campaign, at the very time when GTA was in difficult negotiations to arrange a financial settlement with the Andreas brothers. Andreas sent a $250 check, for which Loriks wrote a thank you on March 20.

Besides the organizational and political matters, Loriks also did some other things during his GTA presidency. One of the things that especially pleased Loriks was that good relationships developed between his organization and South Dakota State University, and its president, Dr. H.M. Briggs. On February 4, 1967, Loriks wrote to Thatcher's secretary, Veronica Boesel, asking that the board at its next meeting "give some recognition to South Dakota State University," pointing out that SDSU was active in feed research and that a number of SDSU alumni were working for GTA. SDSU had also developed a new malting barley.

The GTA Foundation, after Briggs had personally visited Loriks at his farm, gave SDSU a $3,000 gift for the building of the South Dakota Memorial Art Center in Brookings. GTA also gave to other causes, including to the University of South Dakota Continuing Education Center. There were other acts of kindness as well, as there are letters in the Loriks papers from GTA farm families who were helped by the GTA with the paying of hospital and other medical bills. GTA funds also went to education accounts of state Farmers Union organizations and to such groups as the South Dakota Association of Cooperatives.

As Loriks' presidency came to a close, he received many letters of thanks and appreciation. One that he obviously treasured came from Vice President Humphrey, who wrote to thank Loriks for inviting him to the GTA banquet in the fall of 1967. Loriks answered on December 9 by saying, "It is an unprecedented privilege for me to be able to address the Vice President of the United States as my personal friend."

Emil Loriks listens as B.J. "Barney" Mulasky reports to a late 1960s GTA annual meeting. Mulasky became GTA general manager following the retirement of M.W. Thatcher in 1968.
Photo courtesy of South Dakota Farmers Union

On November 27, Loriks wrote lengthy letters to GTA board members with whom he had served, to thank them for the party they gave him at the GTA convention a few days before. "It was a nice party and I want to thank each and everybody who participated, and guess that includes the entire board and their wives." He added, "Want to tell you I especially enjoyed the cooperation I received from you at all times. We did make our influence felt and I feel the outcome of our efforts have been of untold benefit and significance to GTA."

To be sure, Emil Loriks did make his influence felt during his presidency of the GTA—both within the organization itself with its complicated financial and personal affairs, and to the public at large, as a spokesman for GTA and as a representative of the larger Farmers Union. While, in some ways, he perhaps had less direct impact in the GTA presidency than he had as a Farm Holiday organizer or South Dakota Farmers Union president—given the fact that most of the GTA power lay with M.W. Thatcher—he was probably more widely known than he had ever been before, given the regional and even national impact of GTA.

The letters in the Loriks papers indicate that diverse groups and factions within the GTA felt free to express their opinions to Loriks. These letters also suggest a tact and diplomacy on his part in settling the inevitable differences of opinion. The GTA consisted of strong-minded people, M.W. Thatcher representing perhaps the greatest challenge to Loriks' leadership skills, but Loriks met the test. He always focused on the many major achievements of Thatcher's long career in the field of farm legislation and cooperatives. It is probably safe to say that Loriks never lost sight of the big picture as he moved among the day-to-day details of leading the GTA.

As Loriks had correctly pointed out in his last annual report as president, the years of his tenure were a time of expansion. These acquisitions developed a vertical integration of GTA all the way from marketing through processing. GTA was no longer concerned just with the marketing of grain. Loriks had the ability to focus on the larger view of this vertical integration as well as to handle details of difficult internal matters. There were probably some dubious financial arrangements made in the course of the expansion, but Loriks listened to other board members in their questioning of these arrangements and probably was the one who provided the needed counsel and impetus to GTA management to get bad situations resolved.

Loriks was a public figure by virtue of being GTA president, speaking at countless farm meetings over the GTA area, and speaking each year at the GTA annual meeting. The 1967 meeting, according to the Loriks papers, drew 12,000 people. He also spoke at the National Farmers Union convention in 1964 because he was the one who could tactfully express Farmers Union and GTA feelings about national farm policy, without unduly alienating the national administration.

With his retirement as GTA president in November 1967, Loriks' public service career was officially over, although he would continue to write about and speak on issues of public and agricultural concern for the next eighteen years until his death on December 25, 1985. Both Loriks and Thatcher were to die on Christmas Day, Thatcher in 1976, and Loriks, nine years later.

CHAPTER VII

A Career Comes to a Close, 1968-1985

In his final report as president of the GTA, Emil Loriks had said, "Retirement from official position does not mean retirement from service. I shall be working for Farmers Union cooperatives as long as my health permits. I look forward to continued service to these great institutions."

In the last years of his life, then, Loriks, did not really retire from public service. He continued to serve the Farmers Union, which he loved so well, and he continued to speak out on a variety of public issues, especially those related to agriculture, right up to the time he died.

Letters continued to come in to thank him for his service to GTA. Former South Dakota Governor Ralph Herseth wrote in an undated note, "Your record on the GTA board is enviable, also in many other fields. You have added stature in a most admirable manner in all of your endeavors." Roy F. Hendrickson, executive secretary of the National Federation of Grain Cooperatives in Washington, D.C., wrote on November 24, 1967, "As you retire from the GTA board, I want to express my appreciation for the excellent service you have given over the years. You have been steadfast in your support of farmers and their cooperatives. It is your kind of loyalty, wisdom and patience which has helped so greatly in making an idea-dream come true."

Karl Mundt began his letter of December 2 with the Loriks statement cited above about retirement. Mundt continued, "I don't think a better statement could be written defining what your service has been to the farmer and what that concept of service means to you. It's good to know that you will continue to be in there plugging away for American agriculture and I know South Dakota farmers can continue to count on you for your leadership in working to achieve success *for* the farmer, *on* the farm . . . ."

Letters also came from those still in the management of GTA. Loriks would find it a bit difficult to "let go" as some of his letters will show. R.L. Johansen, the GTA public relations director, wrote on November 27, "I want to convey to you my deep appreciation for the many kindnesses and cooperation that you gave me during your tenure as president of the GTA Board. Your friendliness, courtesy and helpfulness will never be forgotten by me. I know too, that when the history of this organization is written, you will be deserving of great credit for the important contributions you have made to its progress over these past 29 years."

B.J. Mulasky, the assistant general manager and the person who would succeed M.W. Thatcher, wrote to Loriks on November 28, "We will miss you at board meetings and I would like to take this opportunity to thank you for the help you have given me over the years and for the many personal favors."

Loriks continued to keep in touch with GTA doings, writing frequent letters to two fellow board members, Ervin Schumacher and Jewell Haaland, who were still on the board after his retirement, and to Norman Olsen of Canton, South Dakota, who succeeded Loriks as a board member from South Dakota. Schumacher wrote on December 16 to tell Loriks that GTA was getting a plaque ready to present to him at the time of the January board meeting. "It would be good if you could *accidentally* be at your daughter's home at that time. Spend one night at the St. Paul hotel and accept the plaque."

Loriks wrote Jewell Haaland, probably early in 1968, to assure him that his letters to him (Loriks) would be kept in confidence. Loriks told Haaland to "keep in close touch with Ehlers [the new GTA president] on important issues, and see that he gets the backing to be effective." Loriks also counseled Haaland that the board should guard against ten-year contracts, which Thatcher was apparently making with personnel, or at least "make sure that such a contract is subject to final approval by the board."

Loriks wrote to Schumacher, expressing concern, in a March 11 letter, about the ten-year contracts in GTA. "How wonderful it would have been if they had backed you and me on that last board meeting in November, when we requested review of each contract by the board before final approval."

Loriks continued to get requests to speak at farm meetings, such as one in Wheaton, Minnesota, on March 7, 1968. The letter of February 2 that asked him to speak in Wheaton, had this postscript: "A lot of us are going to miss you conducting our annual meetings."

Loriks and Thatcher continued to keep in touch and to have warm things to say to each other. In a letter of December 20, 1967, written to the Nebraska Farmers Union president, with a copy sent to Loriks, Thatcher had said of Loriks, "We made our first big expansion during his first year as president in 1958, and many other large ones since then. We simply rebuilt GTA during his ten years of service and cooperation with me."

Apparently the most difficult situation facing the GTA board in the winter and early spring of 1968 was how to effect the retirement of Thatcher. According to one letter Loriks received from a board member, there had even been tentative plans for the board to ask Thatcher to resign.

A letter from another board member to Loriks on January 11 spoke of plans having been made for action against Thatcher at the January 9 board meeting. "We had everything fixed for the grand finale, when some new man was pulled and the T family won again." Thatcher was by this time apparently still running the GTA from his home and not coming to the office—for health reasons. The letter writer went on to hope that Thatcher would soon resign.

By late spring, Thatcher's exit as GTA manager was in place. According to an undated note to Loriks from another GTA board member at the crucial meeting, Thatcher was asked to leave, and the action was taken. "This was the end." Thatcher had apparently wanted a special title and other considerations, but the board did not concur. The same letter said that "Bill cannot have any other place in the annual meeting but the same as any member." The same GTA board member wrote to Loriks on July 2, 1968, "Bill had to get the heave ho—wanted a glorified title on National Front and his General Manager title. Said he was willing to leave details to others—and he would spend his time on important things!"

After the Thatcher retirement, he and Loriks continued to exchange letters, and there are also copies in the Loriks papers of letters written back and forth between Thatcher and other board members, some of the same board members who had helped assure Thatcher's retirement. Thatcher, in a letter of October 27 to Loriks about that fall's campaign, added this sad handwritten postscript, "The next time you are in Minneapolis—hope we can have a visit. GTA is *not* the same. Confidential.—Bill."

The following spring, on April 9, 1969, Thatcher wrote from
Florida again to lament being out of touch with GTA. "Our
relationships and experiences that we shared are much more
satisfying in retrospect than they seemed to be as we lived
through them. Realize that, beginning in 1958 and ending in
1967, GTA experienced its greatest years in foreseeing and
planning and achieving the changes in our marketing problems, which have saved GTA from a disastrous experience."
Thatcher wrote again May 27 to thank Loriks for his "good letter" and to lament his lack of contact with GTA. "Nobody
ever calls me. Apparently GTA is going to lose money for the
year and that will be the first time it ever has. The sad part of
this whole situation, as I see it, is the lack of income to the producers of farm products."

On November 27, Loriks wrote Schumacher a chatty letter,
talking about the GTA annual meeting and about Thatcher,
who did not attend the meeting. "He could really do a sales
job," Loriks wrote of Thatcher. "No one will deny that in his
day, he did a great job of organizing GTA, launching Central
Exchange, Great Plains and putting together the National
Federation of Grain Coops and wielding great influence in
Washington!"

Loriks continued to hear from GTA colleagues, including a
June 2, 1969, note from Schumacher, wondering about GTA's
image. "Can you tell us what good or bad image GTA has in
the country?" the letter asked. It went on, "It seems we have
lost the appeal to younger, unobligated operators." The NFO
was posing a threat. "We will have to resell the coop image and
service to the new generation." Norman Olsen also wrote
Loriks periodically to report on GTA news. Loriks kept in
touch with Barney Mulasky at the GTA office and got
legislative reports from research director Robert Handschin.

Loriks stayed in touch with Schumacher after Schumacher
went off the GTA board. On July 20, 1972, Loriks wrote to
Schumacher to lament that GTA did not have retirement provisions for past board members. "Most of my years on GTA
board, the per diem was $10 a day plus expenses, and the first
year or so I never even collected my per diem because I felt
some sacrifice was necessary in the beginning." In a letter of
the same date to GTA chairman Fred Ehlers, Loriks asked
that the GTA board consider at least carrying some insurance

for retired directors.

There were notes throughout the 1970s, back and forth between Loriks and GTA management. Loriks wrote about legislation in Washington, and on October 12, 1976, wrote to thank GTA manager Barney Mulasky for coming to South Dakota for the Farmers Union convention. Loriks continued to attend GTA annual meetings regularly, doing so up through the 1984 fall meeting. He continued his close contact with Thatcher, until Thatcher's death on December 25, 1976. Loriks kept Thatcher posted on South Dakota political news and encouraged Thatcher in writing his book, which was never completed. Thatcher wrote on November 19, 1973, to wish Ruth and Emil Loriks his best on the occasion of the observance of their fiftieth wedding anniversary that Thanskgiving weekend. "There is nobody in the northwest farm country with whom I have had such friendly and happy relationship as with you folks." In 1976, Loriks loaned Thatcher his copy of John Crampton's study of the Farmers Union, and on June 24, Thatcher wrote to return it with thanks. Loriks wrote back on July 8 to say his book was back, and on October 12, wrote what was probably his last letter to Thatcher to report on the South Dakota Farmers Union convention. "We hope you are well as usual, and we're looking forward to the publication of your book."

Along with all the letter writing that he continued to do, Loriks also found time in his years of "official retirement" to perform other public services. He served on the State Advisory Committee of the Farmers Home Administration, which was the successor to the FSA he had served in the early 1940s.

In an act of personal generosity, he purchased the stately old Peterson house in Oldham when it was for sale in the 1970s and turned it over to the Oldham Museum and Historical Association for its museum. The Loriks-Peterson Heritage House was dedicated on July 4, 1976, as part of the Bicentennial observance. The museum has two rooms of Loriks memorabilia from both Ruth and Emil Loriks. The Loriks papers were first placed in the museum and were termed "a gold mine of material for historians" by South Dakota State University professor Dr. Larry Roberts who inventoried them.

Loriks experienced a great personal sadness when his wife of nearly fifty-four years died on April 19, 1979. Ruth had been in diminishing health for several years—one of the reasons that Emil and Ruth in 1978 had given up living on the farm and moved to a cozy apartment in Oldham.

But even though he was living in town, Emil continued to visit and to work at the farm. In fact, it was his continuing activity at the farm that led to a serious accident in 1980, when he fell from a ladder and spent two months in a Madison hospital recuperating from a major back injury.

Just before he was released from the hospital that fall, a special cake, decorated with a railroad track and switches in

Ruth and Emil Loriks' fiftieth wedding anniversary picture. They celebrated with an open house for family and friends on Thanksgiving weekend of 1973, just a few weeks before the actual January 1974 anniversary date.

Photo courtesy of Ruth Ann Carlson

honor of Loriks' work on behalf of keeping a healthy rail system in South Dakota, arrived at his hospital room. The sender was Governor William Janklow, who was showing his appreciation for Loriks' public and private statements on behalf of the Janklow plan to have the state buy railroad track.

(In the early 1980s, Loriks was somewhat more critical of Janklow on the one issue that was always paramount for Loriks—the ore tax on the Homestake Mine. Governor Janklow concurred with the legislature's action in reducing the Homestake tax levy, after having previously supported a higher level of taxation. In private conversations, Loriks expressed his disappointment with Janklow on this issue, at one point saying indignantly, "I wrote a letter to tell him what I thought and he didn't even answer me!")

In 1981, Loriks received his pin for being a Mason for sixty years, the presentation being made by his sister, Emma Turnquist. Loriks and his World War I flying colleagues, the Silver Wings, continued their annual reunions at the Ellsworth Air Force Base near Rapid City. He often wrote letters on Silver Wings stationery, and in the summer of 1984, he and Glenn Levitt of Clark were flown for a national reunion of flyers in San Antonio. When Eastern Airlines personnel heard that there were two World War I flyers aboard the plane, the airline presented Loriks and Levitt each a bottle of champagne.

The last several falls of his life, Loriks was the subject of governor and local proclamations of Emil Loriks Day in Oldham, with an open house being held outside at the Peterson-Loriks Museum as the weather would permit.

On September 17, 1982, Loriks again made newspaper headlines, as he had ever since he was in the legislature, with his Mercy Food campaign to share the United States abundance of surplus food with the world. The *Argus Leader* story by Chuck Raasch, telling of the Loriks plan, started:

> His fingers prancing through sheets of farm statistics scattered across the kitchen table, 87-year-old Emil Loriks mustered the righteous indignation that had led to last night's farm meeting called by Governor William Janklow.
>
> "We spend so much time to build death-dealing devices," he said, running a hand through a wispy tangle of his oats-colored hair. "It would be better to give something to sustain life."

Executive
Proclamation
State of South Dakota
Office Of The Governor

WHEREAS, Emil Loriks has served the people of South Dakota in both the public and private sectors with distinction and honor; and,

WHEREAS, Emil Loriks has served South Dakotans in numerous capacities, including Administrator of the Federal Farm Program in South Dakota and our Tri-State Region under Franklin Roosevelt; as a member of the South Dakota Railroad Commission; as Senator and Co-chairman of the Appropriations Committee of the South Dakota Legislature; and as an organizer of the Farmers Union Association in South Dakota; and,

WHEREAS, Emil Loriks has served the people of the nation with dedication by protecting our freedoms as a World War I pilot; by helping found the national Farm Holiday Movement; by serving as the national secretary of the Farmers Union Association; and by serving as President of GTA, the largest grain terminal association in the world; and,

WHEREAS, Emil Loriks has dedicated his time and energies to Dakota State College by serving for the past eight years on the Alumni Board of Directors and has been honored by them as the recipient of the Outstanding Alumnus Award and the Distinguished Alumnus Award; and,

WHEREAS, Saturday, October 2, will mark the end of Emil's eight years on the Alumni Board, and the members of the Dakota State College Alumni Board of Directors are conferring the singular honor of naming Emil an honorary member of the board for life, an honor never before given:

NOW, THEREFORE, I, WILLIAM J. JANKLOW, Governor of the State of South Dakota, do hereby proclaim October 2, 1982, as

                              EMIL LORIKS DAY

In South Dakota, and I join the alumni of Dakota State College, the people of South Dakota, and the people of this nation in thanking Emil for his many efforts on our behalf, and especially for choosing to spend his life with us in South Dakota.

IN WITNESS WHEREOF, I have hereunto set my hand and caused to be affixed the Great Seal of the State of South Dakota, in Pierre, the Capital City, this Thirtieth Day of September, in the Year of Our Lord, Nineteen Hundred and Eighty-Two

WILLIAM J. JANKLOW, GOVERNOR

ATTEST:

ALICE KUNDERT, SECRETARY OF STATE

One of many gubernatorial proclamations that honored Emil Loriks.

The Mercy Wheat suggestion by Loriks in 1982 was a direct descendant of a GTA program of 1946 that had been pushed by then-President Harry Truman.

The Raasch piece referred to Loriks' work fifty years before in the Farm Holiday:

> Barely five-foot-six, Loriks is unassuming in a rumpled plaid jacket, plaid top hat and black rimmed glasses. The memory is slower now, but the eyes glow with a passion lit by decades of rural agitation. He walks with a stoop—a testimony to years of farmwork and a broken back a couple of years ago—but he talks with the salt-of-the-earth, common sense style often associated with prairie populists.

The Mercy Wheat plan, endorsed by a wide spectrum of South Dakota farm and political leaders, called for the government to buy up to $4 billion worth of grain from farmers and to channel it through relief and humanitarian agencies to under-developed nations.

Always a prolific writer of letters, Loriks did not stop even in retirement. He kept up his contact with Karl Mundt, speaking out on a variety of issues, not just farm issues. The tone of the letters back and forth between Mundt and Loriks, the one-time political opponents in the bitter race of 1938, was warm. On February 24, 1968, Mundt wrote to say, "It was mighty nice of you to write as you did under date of February 20. It is just unfortunate that the policy of GTA forced your retirement at your most productive age." The letter also reported that "the session has not been productive for farmers so far." On May 3, 1969, he wrote to thank Loriks for "nice words" and to say that "there are indications that our negotiations in Viet Nam may be paying off." He added, "I hope so."

One of Senator Mundt's last major events, before the stroke that effectively ended his senatorial career occurred, was the dedication of the Karl Mundt Library in Madison at Dakota State College in June 1969. Loriks attended the event, which was also attended by President Nixon. Loriks wrote on June 23 to tell Mundt how much he enjoyed the dedication ceremonies. The Viet Nam situation continued to trouble Loriks, as it did so many Americans. "The Viet Nam situation is one that frustrates one's thinking, for it seems that any move we make is wrong. We can't win, and yet we can't hoist the white flag of surrender."

Loriks also carried on a long-standing and extensive correpondence with George McGovern, elected to the Congress from South Dakota in 1956 and 1958, and first elected to the Senate in 1962. The Loriks-McGovern correspondence is as voluminous as the Loriks-Mundt correspondence.

According to the correspondence, Loriks was involved in fund-raising efforts when McGovern ran for Congress in 1956. Loriks continued to support McGovern, including his ill-fated race against Karl Mundt in 1960, which featured two friends of GTA farm policy running against each other.

Right after his victory in the Senate race of 1962, McGovern wrote Loriks on November 24:

> I have just had a wonderful weekend at the home of our dear friend, Bill Thatcher. He speaks very highly of you, and I need not tell you that I share his enthusiasm.
>
> Emil, your help in this campaign was alone enough to have accounted for the margin of victory that we scored.

On January 27, 1964, McGovern wrote, "Dear Emil—I look forward to your notes because you always encourage me." In turn, Loriks wrote to "Dear George," on February 8, to say, "Thank you for the prompt and informative replies to my last two letters. I hope you do not become discouraged in your fight for the voluntary certificate plan for wheat. Even if we do not get everything we want in a bill, it is important that we get it off the ground and perhaps we can improve on it in the process of legislation. It is always a matter of compromises."

Later that year, July 31, McGovern put a handwritten note at the bottom of a note to Loriks. "Your constant high praise is most encouraging to me, Emil. Give me the benefit of your criticism, too."

By May 7, 1967, Loriks wrote to McGovern to talk about political strategy for George McGovern's re-election campaign the next year. Loriks warned in a friendly manner that McGovern would face repercussions because of his strong anti-Viet Nam statements. "Am not telling you anything that you are not already aware of, nor anything unexpected perhaps. So far no great storm brewing, however, am watching developments, if any, in the days ahead."

Letters continued back and forth between Loriks and McGovern throughout McGovern's Senate career, which ended with his defeat by James Abdnor in 1980. Typical of the letters in the 1970s was this one from McGovern on June 10, 1977:

> I certainly enjoyed your recent letter. I wish that you would write me more often.
>
> We had a hard time in the Senate on the Farm Bill, Emil, and I think that we were lucky to come out as well as we did.... For my own part, I feel that we have accommodated the Administration as far as we can and I shall resist all efforts at Senate/House compromise.

William Janklow, South Dakota Governor from 1979-1987, once referred to Loriks as his "pen pal," and that description could probably have been applied by other South Dakota politicians as well. He consistently wrote to congressmen of both parties, including E.Y. Berry, Ben Reifel, Frank Denholm, Larry Pressler and James Abourezk. The subject matter was almost always, but not exclusively, farm policy, as midwestern senators and representatives of both parties tried to forge alliances across party lines to effect favorable farm legislation. More often than not, these politicians and Loriks, along with the GTA and Farmers Union, were at odds with whichever administration was in power, Republican or Democratic.

Loriks also kept up a longstanding correspondence with North Dakota Republican Senator Milton Young. On January 19, 1976, for example, Young wrote to "Dear Emil" to say, "I want to thank you for your nice comment about my work here in the Senate. Your letters have always been encouraging and it seems that our views have almost never differed on the major issues."

Loriks was in contact with Hubert Humphrey throughout Humphrey's term as vice president and after Humphrey returned to the Senate. Humphrey wrote on Senate stationery on March 7, 1973, "Just a note of thanks for your thoughtful and warm message. I hope that I will continue to merit your trust and confidence."

One of Loriks' long standing crusades was that South

Dakota observe Leif Erickson Day, rather than Columbus Day, in view of Loriks' belief that it was the Scandinavian who really discovered North America. He had gotten legislation passed about this concern when he was in the state senate, and wrote every governor since to remind them. Governor Frank Farrar on October 1, 1969, wrote to Loriks to ask him to send a sample proclamation for Farrar to use.

Loriks had an especially warm correspondence with Democratic Governor Richard Kneip who, like Loriks, came from the Arlington area. Governor Kneip was, in fact, one of the mourners at Loriks' funeral service in late December 1985. Throughout Kneip's almost eight years in office, Loriks wrote him both to compliment and to persuade. In March 27, 1971, Loriks wrote to ask Kneip to call a special session of the legislature to deal with the "balanced tax structure" issue. Loriks felt there was bipartisan support for such a move.

Former president Ben Radcliffe presented former president Emil Loriks with the South Dakota Farmers Union Award for Meritorious Service in 1981. The award had been announced at the 1980 state convention, but Emil was hospitalized following a serious back injury and was unable to attend.

Photo courtesy of South Dakota Farmers Union

Emil Loriks and daughter Ruth Ann Carlson stand outside of the family farm home in 1984.

Photo by the author

Kneip did not call such a session, writing to Loriks on April 8 to say that while he was "convinced that South Dakota's tax system desperately needs an overhaul," he did not call the session because "I am equally convinced that although the need is desperate, it would be a waste of money and effort to call a special legislative session without some indication that the majority party is willing to deal with this problem head on."

In his retirement, Loriks stayed in close touch with the South Dakota Farmers Union, attending its conventions every year and often appearing on the program. On October 20, 1976, state president Ben Radcliffe wrote to thank Loriks for his part in the recollections segment of the program.

It is not surprising that Loriks, given his many years of public service to agricultural policy concerns, would be the recipient of many honors. By living past age ninety, Loriks was able to enjoy and receive these honors, instead of having them come posthumously. He was the first recipient of the South Dakota Farmers Union Award for Meritorious Service. In 1979, he was named to the Western Heritage Hall of Fame in Ft. Pierre, and in the summer of 1984, was written up in the Hall of Fame's magazine, *Dakota West.* Loriks served many years on the Dakota State College Board, and in 1982 the college made him a "Lifelong Honorary Member" of that board. In 1971 he had been named the "Distinguished Alumnus of Dakota State College."

He received two honorary doctorates at the end of his life—the first in 1977 from Dakota State College, and the second in 1984 from South Dakota State University, with which he had worked over the years to build a good relationship to aid agriculture. The May 5, 1984, citation read in part, "Agriculturalist, humanist and public servant, Emil Loriks has earned the support, respect and admiration of those whose livelihood is derived from agriculture." The citation referred to his hard work on behalf of water development and railroad preservation and said, "In recognition of a lifetime of dedication to the citizenry of South Dakota, and particularly the farmers and ranchers of this state, South Dakota State University confers on Emil Loriks the degree, Doctor of Public Service."

One of the last honors Loriks received, and one which especially pleased him was to be named to the South Dakota Coop Hall of Fame on October 21, 1985. He and the late Art

Jones of Britton were the first persons to be so honored. Loriks traveled to Mitchell to the banquet at which he was given the award.

One of the high points in Loriks' later life was the interview that author Studs Terkel made with him and his wife, Ruth, for his book about the Great Depression, *Hard Times.* On October 8, 1968, Loriks wrote Terkel a long and friendly letter to say, "We really enjoyed your visit here and reminiscing on Depres-

In 1977 Emil Loriks received an honorary doctorate from his alma mater, Dakota State College at Madison.

Photo courtesy of Ruth Ann Carlson

At the time Emil Loriks was inducted into the Co-op Hall of
Fame in October 1985, former Agriculture Secretary Robert
Berland was the speaker of the evening.

Photo courtesy of South Dakota Farmers Union

sion days!'' On May 25, 1970, Loriks wrote to thank Terkel for
the copy of the book. Right after the interview, Terkel had
written Loriks to thank him for "the good conversations, as
well as Ruth Loriks' exquisite coffee and pastries."

The correspondence continued after the book was published,
Loriks writing Terkel on January 1, 1973, to thank him for the

Christmas greeting. "We often wonder why you happened to select us for the South Dakota interview?" After Loriks' death, Terkel was to comment to the writer during a phone conversation on May 12, 1986, "He represented the wonderful and militant spirit of independent-thinking farmers."

Given Loriks' prominence in the farm cooperative movement and in Upper Midwest farm organizations, beginning in the 1930s, it is also not surprising that he became a key source for broadcast programming on the 1980s that started to examine current farm problems. Closely related, and a proud moment for Loriks, was his being used as an extensive source and on-camera presence for the telecast NBC made in January 1982 to commemorate Franklin Roosevelt's 100th birthday. The camera crews came to the Loriks farm to get their footage, and Loriks could speak with pride of how the New Deal had helped the farmers, forgetting by that time that he had been a somewhat persistent critic of Roosevelt farm policy early in the New Deal, thinking that Roosevelt did not do enough.

On February 18, 1985, Loriks was a key "on mike" source for a Minnesota Public Radio program broadcast nationally on the Farm Holiday, being recalled at that time with special feeling because of the deepening crisis on the farms all across the Midwest. Another major farm program was "Plowing Up a Storm," produced for public television by the Nebraska Educational Television Network, and broadcast for a number of times beginning in June 1985.

Appearing on these regional and national broadcasts perhaps served to make Loriks better known to more people than he had ever been before. The NBC and Nebraska Public Televisions telecasts, in particular, conferred on him celebrity status.

Loriks made good feature material in his retirement years, especially as the 1980s farm crisis brought to mind the parallel developments of the 1930s, with which he was so familiar. One piece which gained wide exposure in the 1970s was a piece by Betty Burg of the Huron Daily *Plainsman* called "Emil Loriks—Family Farm Trailblazer," which was reprinted not only in the *South Dakota Union Farmer*, but in the *Congressional Record* on September 15, 1978, as well, being placed there by Senator McGovern. McGovern called Loriks the "president emeritus of agricultural thought and action in South Dakota." Burg's story began:

You don't have to reach far into the history books to find amazing tales of the pioneers when you have Emil Loriks of Oldham to talk to.

Loriks in his own right has blazed trails in the agricultural sector of South Dakota by working towards a better farm economy during the country's Dust Bowl years.

In 1980, Loriks was featured by AP writer Tena Andersen for recalling the Legislature of the 1930s. In 1981, *Argus Leader* reporter Chuck Raasch featured Loriks as a "champion of South Dakota." Wrote Raasch, "Although his World War I fighter pilot's reflexes might have slipped with age, 86-year-old Emil Loriks remains a battler—mostly for railroads and his home state of South Dakota" (*Argus Leader,* July 26, 1981).

On February 22, 1983, Loriks was the subject of a feature in the Brookings *Daily Register:* "Oldham native reservoir of history, politics." The story concluded by saying that "Although Loriks isn't in the political spotlight anymore, his views are often valued and he is greatly admired by other politicians." Representative Tom Daschle was quoted on Loriks, "A person who has lived history as Emil, a person who possesses the wealth of knowledge that he has, offers a great deal of advice and guidance to the elected officials of our state."

In the fall of 1984, Loriks was the subject of official proclamation, and also of two public programs about 1930s farm events. Governor William Janklow declared September 30-October 6 as Emil Loriks Week, using these words as part of his citation: "Carl Emil Loriks has served the people of South Dakota and the United States with great distinction: Emil's accomplishments include the founding of the Farm Holiday movement, the original organizing of the Farmers Union in South Dakota, the passage of the state's first gold tax, and the reduction of state government expenditures by 25 percent during the first years of the Great Depression." The proclamation made additional references to his being a legislator, being co-chair of the Appropriations Committee, and administrator of a federal farm program, and being president of the GTA.

The two meetings that fall, "Emil Loriks: Agrarian Exponent," took place in Brookings and in Huron, with sponsorship by the South Dakota Committee on the Humanities, the South

One of the highlights of the 1976 South Dakota Farmers Union state convention was the participation of four past presidents in a bicentennial program on Farmers Union history. Seated are Paul Opsahl (1947-1958) and Emil Loriks (1934-1938). Standing are Ben Radcliffe (1961-1981), Oscar Fosheim (1944-1947) and John Skage (1938-1944).

Photo courtesy of South Dakota Farmers Union

Dakota State University Speech Department, the South Dakota Farmers Union and GTA Feeds.

Loriks had promised on his retirement from GTA to continue to serve, which is exactly what he did from 1968 to the end of 1985. That service was also widely recognized toward the end of his long and productive life—he got the pleasure of receiving many awards and reading about his life. His counsel was still sought by South Dakota political leaders.

Emil Loriks, October 1984, makes a point during one of the Humanities Committee-sponsored meetings about his life.
Photo courtesy of South Dakota Farmers Union

CHAPTER VIII

Emil Loriks: Prairie Persuader

A large measure of Emil Loriks' public service career consisted of persuasion. Every letter he wrote was part of that persuasion, and the other major component, which merits a detailed look, is in his many speeches. The very nature of his positions—legislator, Farm Holiday organizer, Farmers Union president, political candidate, federal administrator and GTA president—meant that he gave a large number of speeches. Moreover, his public speaking continued throughout his retirement; between 1968 and 1985 he spoke to farm organization

Emil Loriks testifies at a January 30, 1968, tax hearing in the House chambers in Pierre. Farmers Union members crowded the gallery for the hearings.

Photo courtesy of South Dakota Farmers Union

Even after he retired, Loriks continued to attend GTA annual meetings as an active participant. He speaks from the floor at an early 1970s GTA annual meeting.

Photo courtesy of South Dakota Farmers Union

meetings, to sessions of the Dakota history conferences, to political gatherings, and to college and university classes.

One can gain a look at Loriks' persuasive practices because a large number of his speeches have been saved. His papers contain either notes, working copies or final drafts of many speeches, and all the speeches he gave over WNAX in Yankton during the time he was state Farmers Union president are on file at South Dakota Farmers Union headquarters in Huron. His South Dakota Farmers Union presidential addresses given to the fall conventions are on file as part of the convention reports at Farmers Union headquarters.

Another major component of his persuasive efforts was the annual reports that he gave while he was GTA president. These, too, are a part of the written and preserved record.

As a beginning to developing a statement about Loriks' persuasive practices, the writer had the opportunity to interview both Loriks, himself, and his daughter, Ruth Ann Carlson, on July 19, 1982. Mrs. Carlson cited several characteristics of her father as being instrumental in his approach to persuasion. She called her father "very sincere" and one "who liked people." He would recognize the needs of others and try to offer solutions. Moreoever, he "had boundless energy and went day and night." Mrs. Carlson added that his "good speaking voice and intelligence" were also factors in his persuasive efforts. A letter written on March 18, 1955, by the manager of an elevator association in Salem to which Loriks had spoken, bears these comments out: "It seems like no matter how late it gets or how tired they are when you get up to speak, you do something for them."

Both Mrs. Carlson and Loriks, himself, felt that his sense of identification with his audience was crucial to his persuasive efforts. "He was one of the farmers and knew their problems firsthand. They trusted him," she said. Loriks also referred to this same sense of identification by saying that he had "sensed the lack of representation that agriculture had." He added, "As a farmer, I knew what their needs and their gripes were." This sense of identification with farm needs is what led Loriks into politics and public service. "I had the feeling that farmers weren't adequately represented and that they had an inferiority complex." Loriks added that knowing rural needs and having ideas about what could be done about these problems were keys to his persuasion.

The interview with Mrs. Carlson and Loriks also uncovered another key to his persuasive efforts—persistence. Mrs. Carlson said, "Along with persuading, he was always encouraging people." Loriks was not one to give up easily in a difficult situation, according to his daughter. She said to her father directly during the interview, "You didn't back off, you didn't easily give up," and went on to recall that her father had not gotten discouraged when he lost to Karl Mundt in 1938, but that by comparison, his good friend Oscar Fosheim, who lost the Democratic race for governor that year, had.

Both Loriks and his daughter indicated that Loriks' approach went beyond simply giving a speech on a topic. She referred to his vast volume of letter writing, and to his use of the telephone. Loriks recalled that in his Farmers Union organizing days, he would travel to help organize local farm groups and cooperatives. His daughter added that these meetings would be followed up by resolutions and the writing of letters to congressmen. The degree of Loriks' personal commitment to his cause is reflected in the fact that when he was Farmers Union state president, he would travel as much as 50,000 or 60,000 miles a year.

Part of Loriks' skill and success at persuasion had to be attributed to the fact that he liked to communicate with people. Even as a boy, "He always did like to talk," Emma Turnquist, his sister, said to this writer early in 1985.

Several characteristics of Loriks' rhetoric can be identified, especially from his speeches in the days of his Farmers Union presidency. One characteristic was the use of what speech scholars would call emotional proof—appealing to the emotions of listeners. Examples of this abound in the "early eulogy" speech given on September 9, 1935, over WNAX, right after Loriks had heard of Huey Long's being shot, but before his death was confirmed. He said of Long, "*Today,* the outstanding friend of the downtrodden, the exploited, the destitute, lies at death's door, the victim of the bloody hand of an assassin." Calling Long, "Most misrepresented, maligned and persecuted of statesmen today by the powerful interests that rule this nation because he dared to attack the evils at their source, [he] has been shot down in cold blood by the reeking, smoking pistol in the purpled hands of an assassin."

Closely tied to the use of emotional proof were the examples of scapegoating, particularly of the Homestake Mine, against which Loriks battled in the gold tax fight. Loriks labeled that interest as one of the major causes of ills confronting farmers of that day. In his presidential address to the Farmers Union convention in 1936, Loriks began the attack in general terms against the capitalistic system. "Capitalism has long been compared to the slot machine. He who plays the slot machine long enough will inevitably go broke. The profit system has already busted most of us. It has put us down in the economic gutter." Loriks focused his attack, "*We* have had a taste of it in South Dakota—how the dominant economic interest [the Hearst-Homestake Mining Interest] situated in one county has dominated our state for half a century."

The attack on Hearst and Homestake continued with these words:

> Today we behold Hearst in the role of America's Fascist No. 1 with the largest newspaper empire in the world to promote the selfish avaricious cause of a decadent capitalism. Hearst is leading America down the road to Fascism, to capitalistic dictatorship.
>
> South Dakota is helping to nourish these beasts whose tentacles reach into every corner of our land. Do you know that they are sucking $18 to $19 million out of one gold mine in South Dakota annually? More than Jefferson paid Napoleon for the entire Louisiana Purchase, every year taken out of one gold mine in South Dakota. Do you know that this gold is helping to nourish the Hearst Octopus to finance his poison propaganda to be spread through the columns of the largest newspaper empire in the world plus a large national chain of broadcasting stations Hearst owned? You members of the Farmers Union, when you fought the Hearst Homestake interests, were not fighting just a local enemy—you were fighting the biggest menace to democracy in America today. Your fight was just a skirmish on one front.

The Hearst-Homestake epithet was to recur in a speech Loriks gave in 1938, in his capacity as South Dakota Farmers Union President on April 28, over the National Farmers Union Radio Hour, broadcast by NBC from Chicago. In this radio talk, Loriks spent considerable time discussing the need for farm legislation, and said, "Bills that are of real benefit to the masses of people, if they touch the economic interests, will meet with terrific opposition." He then told the story of the gold tax battle with Homestake in the South Dakota legislature in 1935. "The people won a glorious victory," he said. Equating economic power with political power, Loriks went on in this national radio address to state emphatically, "Powerful economic interests oppose all social and economic reform, resulting in the deadlock of parliamentary democracy, and consequent inaction. Like Nebuchadnezzar of old, they cannot read the handwriting on the wall."

Attacks on large economic interests can be found again in a speech that Loriks made in 1962, while president of the GTA at a grain meeting in Brady, Montana: "If we permit corporations, chains and monopolies to take over our economy and dominate our political life, then our hopes for survival will indeed go glimmering." But for all this apparent radicalism, Loriks in the same speech, as he did on so many other occasions, offered cooperatives as the solution—basically a way of working within the system, and not of tearing it down. "To counteract this unhealthy concentration of wealth, we have cooperatives, the democratic way. That is why cooperatives have been referred to as the engines of democracy and free enterprise." Loriks indeed laid heavy blame on corporate economic interests—they were his frequent scapegoats. This was often done in an emotional way, and not even without a little name calling, as exemplified by frequent references to "Hearst-Homestake" interests. It is worth noting that Loriks' annual reports as GTA president do not employ the scapegoating techniques he used in the Farmers Union rhetoric of the 1930s.

Another ingredient in Loriks' persuasive philosophy was to make frequent calls for loyalty to the farm group for which he was speaking. He coupled this with frequent emphasis on the cooperative nature of the Farmers Union and GTA. In the 1936 convention speech, Loriks emphasized the Farmers Union's full name—"The Farmers Educational and Cooperative Union." He referred to the building of cooperatives across the state. "We are essentially producers and we are also the chief consumer," he said. "The cooperators who think in terms of building a new economic interest are possessed of vision.

They are the ones who will ultimately change society."

Loriks also made frequent reference to being a "buck private," even when he was a farm leader. In this 1936 speech, he said, "As a 'buck private' in the cooperative movement, I have always adhered to this philosophy [to cooperatives], call it blind unreasoning loyalty if you will, that I will market through my coop and buy my supplies through my coop regardless of the chiseling tactics of the opposition. . . . I am helping to build a New Economic Order."

In his written annual GTA reports, Loriks also emphasized loyalty to the cooperative philosophy and to GTA. In 1960, he wrote, "In closing, let me say that as we come into a period of great changes, GTA's chances of surviving as a cooperative, essential to the family farmer, will depend on several things. I want to stress loyalty, but demands cannot be made on loyalty unless the people understand what is at stake and are ready to work together to achieve their ends."

Closely related was the Loriks characteristic of inspirational appeals. In the 1936 convention address, Loriks concluded with these words:

> Let us concentrate on further legislative victories in the next session, but let us not forget to build a new economic system, a new economic system through cooperative efforts.
>
> *Let us continue to remind ourselves of the fundamental principles for which the Farmers Union was founded.*

In the final WNAX broadcast he made as president of the state Farmers Union in 1938, Loriks ended the talk on an inspirational note (printed in July 20, 1938, *South Dakota Union Farmer*):

> Not only are we gaining in membership, but our cooperative volume has increased just about 100 percent over 1937. Let us all work just a little harder and let us make 1938 a banner year. . . . This is my last radio broadcast as your state president, and I assure you that as a "buck private" my interest in the organization shall not diminish. Let us continue to build our organization bigger and better.

Loriks also made skillful use of repetition as a speaking

technique. In the 1938 national Farmers Union broadcast, he combined inspirational appeals with repetition. This speech had perhaps the most clearly organized structure of any Loriks speech. After the introduction, in which he referred to vast technological changes of the past fifty years, in which he cited examples from his own life, Loriks presented his theme, "It's up to you and me." (The choice of theme resulted from Loriks' having visited with the national president about what he should say and having been told, "It's up to you.") "It's up to you and me—the solution of our economic problems." Loriks detailed the Farmers Union legislative programs and its approach to cooperative marketing. There was an attack, already cited, on the Hearst-Homestake interest. He appealed to his audience to further organize the Union and ended by saying:

> When we look across the waters, you and I should be happy that we still have the opportunity here in America to solve our economic problems in a peaceful way without violence, bloodshed or sacrifice of human lives! Let us keep faith with the founders of our democracy. Let us keep faith with "our buddies in Flanders field." Let us preserve that great tradition of American liberty and democracy and make it a living reality.

Another component of Loriks' rhetoric was to build audience support by stressing the accomplishments of his cause.

In his 1960 GTA president's annual report, Loriks spent considerable time detailing GTA accomplishments of that year, including the building of new elevators, the purchase of other elevator companies, and the acquisition of the Honeymead plant. He discussed the nature of GTA expansions, first noting that the new ventures "are being enthusiastically supported," and that they "have not been taken on any sudden impulse. They reflect much careful consideration and study by your Board of Directors."

The concluding words of the report were:

> But we must not let our pride paralyze us. It is a demonstration of what farm people can do. . . . GTA was not built by timid souls, nor by those who are fearful of the future and believe only in maintaining the past. GTA was built by men of vision and

courage, with a determination to go forward, to
move ahead, to keep abreast with the new era. . . .
This may seem like a bold vision, but its success is
likely to depend on how well each of us do our part in
planting the idea of peace through abundance in our
own land, so that the world can reap the harvest.

Similar persuasive technique can also be found in Loriks'
1961 annual GTA report. Noting that he had served on the
GTA board of directors since 1940, he listed expansions under-
taken by GTA since the start of his presidency, and noted the
major growth in the organization's net worth. "In 1958 we
entered upon the most ambitious program of expansion and
development in our history. We haven't stopped yet."

In the 1961 report, Loriks also emphasized the importance of
the political process in bringing about better farm prices. "We
must have a political, as well as economic awareness. We must
know how to use our coops. And, above all, we must understand that farm prices are made in Washington."

The report ended with these inspirational paragraphs:

We must find ways to use this nation's enormous
productive agricultural capacity to provide for an
expanded abundant life in other nations, as well as
in our own nation.

Our agricultural resources can be weapons for
peace. We can substitute the tools of production for
the tools of destruction. . . .

All of the new facilities and new buildings, as well
as the new plans that are now underway at GTA, are
only for one purpose, to help farm people. This
philosophy of cooperative service and cooperative
help is strong enough to help people everywhere.
Everyone in the world can benefit from the coop
way.

In his final report to the GTA, after ten years of being president, Loriks outlined his lifetime of involvement with farm
issues, noting that his work with GTA had started thirty years
before, when he and other Upper Midwest Farmers Union
presidents had met with M.W. Thatcher to help launch the
GTA in 1937. He then listed GTA accomplishments, noting
GTA growth and volume of business. "When we began, it took

only a small room in a St. Paul hotel to handle our meetings. Now we use the St. Paul Auditorium and bring thousands to our sessions.''

Loriks' persuasive efforts were rooted in a sincere interest in other people and in a sense of identification with the needs of his farm audiences. Not only was there a sense of personal involvement and identification in Loriks' persuasive efforts, but there was also a certain persistence. He did not stop with making a speech or helping to organize a Farmers Union local or a cooperative; these efforts were followed up by resolutions and letters. This persistence, it seems reasonable to conclude, was a reflection of a deep commitment to his cause.

Particularly in his speeches of the 1930s, during the depths of Depression-era agrarian unrest and protest, Loriks tended to use emotional appeals and was not above scapegoating. His favorite scapegoat was the Homestake gold mine in Lead—and the battle he carried on in the South Dakota legislature in 1935 to get the ore tax enacted. More than one Loriks speech contained references to "Hearst-Homestake" interests, and there were frequent general attacks against large corporations, which Loriks held responsible for the farmers' plight. The use of scapegoats was not unusual for agrarian protest rhetoric of that day.

Still other ingredients of the Loriks persuasive mix included calls to loyalty to his farm groups, a tendency to speak in inspirational terms, and the use of repetition to make his points. One other device used to gain credibility was for him to list the accomplishments of the farm group he was heading. He also listed his own long personal involvement with agricultural issues by referring to his own legislative service, the Farm Holiday movement, the Farmers Union and the GTA. The sense of identification that Loriks felt with farm groups was probably deliberately emphasized through such personal references.

Some of the influences on Loriks' persuasive practices can be seen in his early life. Loriks, in the July 19, 1982, interview, recalled his home as one "where they talked about things." He recalled that his father was a Republican, but one sympathetic to the Nonpartisan League. The Loriks family also probably attended Chautauquas in the area, according to what Mrs. Carlson remembered her father having said.

Another major influence on Loriks' persuasive strategies

was his considerable debate and other extra-curricular activity experience at Eastern Normal. Alice Lorraine Daly was a key figure not only in helping to shape the young Loriks' political beliefs, but also his persuasive techniques. All of the debate, theater and yearbook experience brought him in contact with people and that meant that he was trying to persuade them served him well in later years.

Loriks' experience in teaching, both in Alma, Nebraska, and later at the country school near Oldham, also gave him practice in persuading and leading others.

When his own family was established, his was a home where ideas were discussed. Ruth Ann Carlson recalled that he would come home from political or farm meetings to talk. She also recalled, in the same July 1982 interview, that he was "very positive in his approach."

Another great influence on Loriks' persuasion, and one which continued throughout his life, was his extensive reading. Daughter Ruth Ann recalled after her father's death that their home always had a lot of magazines around including not only the Farmers Union publications, which one would have expected to find in this farm leader's home, but also a host of others. He read a number of daily newspapers and also the *Farm Journal* and *U.S. News,* which he considered fairer than *Time,* "which he refused to read," Ruth Ann said. She also remembered *Look, Life, Saturday Evening Post,* and *Successful Farming* being in their home, as well as the *Congressional Record.* There also would be a Swedish paper or two, which Loriks was, of course, able to read directly in Swedish.

Ruth Ann also recalled that he always bought magazines when he traveled. One book which particularly moved him was John Steinbeck's *Grapes of Wrath,* the story of the Depression era movement of the Okies to California.

Loriks showed persuasive and leadership qualities in at least one other way. He was president of his rural congregation, the Spring Lake Evangelical Covenant Church, located near his farm and northeast of Oldham, for many years.

The influences on Loriks' longtime persuasive efforts were diverse. The beginnings were in his family life while he was growing up, and were later reinforced in his own family. The fruition came at Eastern Normal, where Loriks, "who always did like to talk," participated in debate, the literary society and in journalism. A prime influence at Madison—who encouraged the young Loriks to become interested in the world around him and who helped to shape his persuasive efforts—was coach and teacher Alice Lorraine Daly. The difference between Loriks and most college debaters was that he went on to spend a lifetime engaged in persuasive activities—letters, meetings, resolutions and speech making and report writing.

Certainly one of Loriks' key attributes was his considerable ability to persuade others.

CHAPTER IX

A Final Word

A few months before his death on Christmas Day 1985, Emil Loriks attended the huge February 12 Farm Rally in Pierre. The rally, like the later trip by the entire South Dakota Legislature to Washington, D.C., had as its purpose to dramatize the increasingly difficult economic situation facing farmers. After the farmers had rallied on the Capitol steps and marched through part of Pierre, they gathered at the Riggs Auditorium for a long afternoon of speech making. Governor William Janklow introduced Loriks to the crowd, calling him, "the heart of rural America—and he has been since the 1930s." According to Janklow, the ovation given to Loriks was the largest of the day.

Loriks lived his life as a strong exponent of the cooperative system for farmers—the cooperative buying of their supplies, the cooperative marketing of their products, and cooperation to develop the services such as electricity and telephone that they needed. A long speech that Loriks gave to an October 15, 1959, Region 6 Telephone meeting at Huron provides many clues to his beliefs about cooperatives. His topic was "Do We Need More Cooperation," which he, not surprisingly, answered in the affirmative. He carefully sketched the history of cooperative rural telephone systems, pointing out that even in 1959, only 49 percent of all homes in the north central area had dial phones. "There is a lot of room for growth," he remarked. Loriks termed the dwellers of cities much more fortunate in the matter of phone service, pointing out that vast rural distances and decreasing numbers of farmers tended to make expansion of phone service in rural areas much more expensive.

"We can't hope to get service to most farms yet unserved, except by more cooperatives," he said. In looking at cooperation as a whole, he noted that cooperative buying of supplies by farmers was much more extensive than cooperative marketing of their goods.

A major theme of this Loriks speech was the increasing

bigness of American society. "This leads many to wonder if the challenge of the next ten years is whether farmers can do their own integration and thus keep their independence, or whether middlemen will come to control most of the farming operation. Can coops grow fast enough and in the right ways to give their members the advantages of integration?" Speaking prophetically, he added, "If so, the family type of farms will have a good chance to survive, but if not, then our farms will decline into absentee management, a scheme which in the past has always ended in disaster for those societies which allowed it to happen."

The theme of Loriks' entire public service career was summed up in these words near the end of his speech. "If we don't have more cooperation, then family farming will give way to domination by corporations and larger landed interests, bringing in a new kind of rural America, the kind in fact which most of our forefathers came to this country to escape."

Certain unifying strains emerge from Loriks' life. At the funeral service in the small and very warm-hearted Evangelical Covenant Church northeast of Oldham, just a short distance from the family farm he loved so much, one of the pastors who preached identified three Loriks traits.

The first was his "concern and involvement in the needs of people—particularly those with little economic power," Pastor Conrad Krahling said. As this book has tried to demonstrate, Loriks spent his life battling what he perceived as the big and the bad, and advocating the case of those who were less fortunate. Emil was himself a man of very comfortable means; he would not have needed to do that. He could have stayed close to his farm, enjoying the material benefits of his holdings and his operations.

The second quality of which Pastor Krahling spoke was "Emil's desire to learn and his concern for education." Just two weeks before his death, Emil had been asked about his thoughts on the Biblical Jubilee Year, in which every fiftieth year, all would return to their families and their property, and all debts would be forgiven. "He was very much interested and was going to study those chapters," Krahling said. "I was looking forward to hearing his thoughts." Former Lake Preston *Times* editor John Sittner, in writing a letter on November 12, 1982, to support Loriks as a candidate for an honorary doctorate from South Dakota State University, spoke of that concern for education. We recalled a conversation that he had had with Loriks about the GTA scholarship program. Sittner wrote of his long association with Loriks, "His struggle for the family farm has been geared to preservation of our rural sociology, of which the securing of educational opportunties for farm youth has been a major part." One must remember, too, that one side of the Farmers Union triangle is education, along with legislation and cooperation.

Krahling identified a third Loriks characteristic, "his lack of bitterness and hatred." Loriks was involved in some passionate political battles in his day—the gold severance tax campaign and the 1938 race against Karl Mundt being only two examples. The hundreds of letters between Karl Mundt and Emil Loriks as they subsequently pursued their common goal of a better farm policy testify that there was no lasting bitterness. In staying cheerful, Loriks was somewhat unique from some other 1930s agrarians. SDSU historian John Miller has said that others became bitter or left the public arena altogether, but Loriks did not retreat or turn inward.

It seems safe to say that the tap root of Loriks' concern for other people, his cheerful disposition and his lifelong public service was found in his religious faith. This was not something that he bragged about, or even talked about much. The Evangelical Covenant Church back in Sweden had resulted from a break with the state Lutheran Church of Sweden. A pamphlet called "Covenant Church at Glance," describes the denomination by saying that it "has its roots in historical Christianity as it emerged in the Protestant Reformation, in the Biblical instruction of the Lutheran State Church of Sweden, and in the great spiritual awakening of the 19th Century." The church sees as its two tasks, "evangelism and Christian nurture," and draws a distinction between "personal freedom" and "individualism that disregards the centrality of the Word of God and the mutual responsibilities, and discipline of the spiritual community." Loriks put great store on these "mutual responsibilities."

His parents were among the founders of the Spring Lake Evangelical Covenant Church, the immediate impetus for the founding of the church in 1893 having been the refusal of a Lutheran pastor to bury a family member. Loriks served as chairman of the congregation for many years, sometimes writing to thank those who had moved away from the rural community for their continued support of that church. A letter of December 31, 1970, written to a serviceman and his wife then in New Jersey, said, "You are two in a million to be so thoughtful and considerate. Can assure you it will be appreciated exceedingly."

One of the last things Loriks did before his death was to send the Spring Lake pastor (the church by then being serviced on only an occasional basis by Pastor John Haag of Lake Norden) a check for the church's work. In the 1930s, Emil had carried water to nurture the evergreens in the church cemetery; those very trees formed the backdrop for his interment on a cold but clear late December day.

Even though Loriks spent relatively little time as a classroom teacher (although his many roles as a farm leader certainly meant he was a teacher in the broad sense of the word), those students lucky enough to have him as an instructor remember him fondly. Halvor Stenson, who had lived with the Loriks family as a young man when he worked as a hired hand on their farm, had Loriks as his teacher for only a week. Stenson's eighth grade year in his own school finished before the term in Emil's school ended in 1921-22, so Stenson attended Emil's school briefly. Years later, Stenson wrote about that experience:

> He was one of the most remarkable, natural born teachers that I think I ever had. The pupils in his school respected him and really loved him because he seemed to be able to understand them and teach them as perhaps no other teacher they had could do. He could teach history and geography and literature so you literally lived the lives of the great men and women he told about. He did not use traditional teaching methods, but developed his own most interesting and effective teaching methods.

That ability to teach and to touch others was also closely linked to his sense of history. Not only did he refer to history as he led farm groups and movements; he also surely had a sense of history in saving his volumes of papers and in so freely sharing his life and words with the many who came to interview him in his later years.

Loriks was also a good friend. Even though most of his letters over the years dealt with agricultural and political business, there were often personal references and notes of thanks. On one occasion, Ervin Schumacher of North Dakota had sent a kangaroo belt to Emil after his trip to Australia. On February 19, 1967, Loriks wrote to Schumacher, "Now I have something to hold my pants up with." More than one letter talked in personal terms about the always threatening South Dakota farm enemy—drought. On July 7, 1949, he wrote to August Dahme, "One farm completely hailed out for me, and it is now summer fallowed. It sure has been hot. No rain down our way and very dry."

One of his longest and deepest friendships was with Glenn Levitt, whom he met while both were training as World War I

Emil was a proud member of veterans' organizations. In this late 1970s picture, he displays his World War I uniform.

Photo courtesy of Huron *Daily Plainsman*

pilots. (They had grown up on farms only a few miles apart, but the Levitt family "traded" in Arlington and the Loriks family in Oldham, so they did not meet until they both got to Texas.) On July 8, 1976, Loriks wrote his good friend, a couple of years his senior, and quoted the words of his granddaughter, "Of all your friends, I think the Levitts are the nicest." Unlike so many of his associations and friendships, the bond with Glenn Levitt was not political; Levitt was an ardent Republican. In a

Emil in his American Legion cap.
Photo courtesy of Madison *Daily Leader*

February 1986 interview with the author, he indicated that the two early on had agreed not to discuss politics. They both treasured their association with the Silver Wings of World War I, writing letters back and forth on Silver Wings stationery, and looked forward to their annual reunion trips to Ellsworth Air Force Base.

Loriks did not seem to have enemies, at least long-lasting enemies. (It may have helped that he outlived as many political antagonists as he did!) The lack of bitterness, already referred to, is a key reason why he did not seem to have enemies.

Part of his appeal, too, was his sincerity and the sense he conveyed of being quite ordinary. On one of the author's visits to Oldham to visit with people about Loriks, one of the older ladies whom she interviewed, who had known the family since Emil was a baby, said emphatically, "I do not see anything out of the ordinary about him." He really was somewhat extraordinary, but he didn't seem that way.

Loriks, who always spoke with a heavy Swedish accent, was quick with a phrase, not being above occasional demagoguery in some of his oratory about the Homestake Mine. For years after the 1935 enactment of the gold ore tax, Homestake Mine remained his favorite villain in his speeches, often being so described in highly emotional terms. At the same time, there would be many historical allusions and references, reflecting his extensive reading. One should not be misled by the seemingly emotional excess, without looking also at the actions, and also the vast body of letters. Here, former South Dakota Farmers Union President Ben Radcliffe's assessment that "Emil Loriks was both a leader and a stabilizer in the Farmers Union and the GTA" applies. Radcliffe added in an interview with the author on January 7, 1985, "He knew how to be aggressive and outspoken without alienating others who might not agree with him."

Emil's family no doubt wished that he had spent more time at home on the farm, his Farmers Union and GTA travels, not to mention his FSA job, taking him away for long segments of time. Bob Handschin, who first got to know Emil when he, Handschin, was working as a lobbyist in Washington, D.C., in the late 1930s and early 1940s before he went back to St. Paul to work for the GTA, recalled in late 1986 a story that illustrates the blending of Emil's public and private lives. The Handschins had invited Emil, during one of his farm politicking trips to the capital, to come by their small apartment for dinner. Emil arrived, after a day of testifying on Capitol Hill, carrying a pink parasol under his arm. When he was asked what it was for, he replied that the parasol was for his daughter Ruth Ann, by that time nine or ten years old. Emil seemed completely oblivious to the stares and comments he had probably engendered while carrying the parasol around all day.

Loriks is remembered as a generous person who cared about others. But he was not much prone to spend money on himself. His father had sent him off to school at Madison with $10 and a wish of good luck. His family apparently had to urge him to spend money on himself and his carrying of his paychecks around in his pocket during FSA days and not cashing them promptly is indicative of his lack of concern about himself, and his concern for taking care of others.

Emil could advocate unpopular views in a sometimes hostile setting. Bill Dunn, Madison *Daily Leader* reporter, in his December 30, 1985 tribute, described how he had been with Loriks at a meeting of a military service organization when the proposed nuclear freeze vote was on the agenda. A motion was made to express disapproval and was about to be passed, when Loriks got up to say, "Wait a minute. I think we ought to know what we're voting about. Just what does this thing really say?"

In a letter to the author on February 6, 1986, Chuck Raasch, the former Sioux Falls *Argus Leader* reporter who had written so much about Loriks during his tenure in Sioux Falls, said, "In my work there, Loriks was one of a handful of South Dakotans who really touched me. One can become cynical with all the shallow, pop personalities that seem to flash through today's celebrity-oriented mass media, but Emil was all humanity. I never once got the feeling that he was talking to me to make his own star shine brighter." He was totally uncynical.

Loriks' life of public service is a story worth telling. His leadership in trying to better the life of South Dakota and Midwestern farmers was firmly rooted in the American system. At times sounding like a radical, or even an agitator, he really sought to reform the system to make it work better—not to destroy it. Leader and stabilizer, both.

In Chuck Raasch's words in the December 27, 1985 *Argus Leader:* "As much as anyone, he lived the history of the state he so dearly loved. Here was a man with a story. As important as his story was, he'll perhaps be remembered more for how he told it: grandly, proudly, with spirit.''

Emil holds Governor William Janklow's proclamation for the final Emil Loriks Day in Oldham in October 1985.

Emil and his daughter, Ruth Ann, at his final birthday, his ninetieth, on July 18, 1985.

Emil and Ruth Ann, taken in October 1985.

The special cake for Emil Loriks Day, October 6, 1985.

Emil Loriks, in his ever-present hat, continues his life-time practice of reading and doing research to support a political cause dear to his heart.

Photo courtesy of Sioux Falls *Argus Leader*

Bibliographic Essay

Chapter I

The early background about the Loriks family is based on conversations with Emil Loriks and his daughter, Ruth Ann Carlson. In addition, Loriks gave a paper called "Early Pioneers around Oldham" at the 15th Annual Dakota History Conference on April 7, 1983, in which he described immigrant settlements in that area. Herbert E. Schell's *History of South Dakota* (3rd edition) is the source of material about South Dakota land and also for statewide election results in 1926. Halvor Stenson, who worked for and lived with the Loriks family as a young man, provided anecdotal material as did Loriks' former student Eleanor Johnson of Oldham. The 1922 election results came from "Election Record #2, Kingsbury County," available at the County Auditor's office in DeSmet. Data about Loriks' unsuccessful run for state superintendent of public instruction in 1924 were found in the 1925 *South Dakota Manual.* The election results for the 1926 Kingsbury County state senate race were found in "Election Record #2." The Eastern Normal College yearbook, the *Anemone,* in its 1915 and 1916 editions, tells about Loriks' college life and about Alice Lorraine Daly. Homer Ayres, West River South Dakota rancher and long a spokesman for radical agrarian causes, recalled Daly's association with him and his father during a conversation with the author in August 1985. Lowell K. Dyson's *Red Harvest: The Communist Party and American Farmers* provided information on radical farm politics.

Chapter II

Information about the economic conditions in the 1920s and 1930s was drawn from a variety of historians. These included *American Epoch* by Arthur Link and *The Age of Roosevelt: The Coming of the New Deal* by Arthur M. Schlesinger, Jr.

Several historians and economists have written about the agricultural side of the Great Depression. These works cited in the chapter include *Cornbelt Rebellion: The Farmers' Holiday Association* by John L. Shover and *Agricultural Discontent in the Middle West* by Theodore Saloutos and John D. Hicks.

The sources for the South Dakota historical information include Herbert S. Schell's *History of South Dakota* (3rd edition) and Robert Karolevitz's *Challenge: The South Dakota Story*. Two invaluable sources of information about the South Dakota Farmers Union and the South Dakota Farm Holiday of the 1930s are Robert Thompson's "The History of the South Dakota Farmers Union," his master's thesis at the University of South Dakota, 1953, and John Miller's analytical study, "Restrained, Respectable Radicals: The South Dakota Farm Holiday," which was published in *Agricultural History* in July 1985.

Letters cited in the text were found in the Loriks papers. Speeches made while Loriks was an officer of the South Dakota Farmers Union are on file at South Dakota Farmers Union headquarters in Huron. Reference was also made to a September 1978 article, "Emil Loriks: Family Farm Trailblazer," that appeared in the *South Dakota Union Farmer*, official newspaper of the South Dakota Farmers Union. Interviews by the author of Emil Loriks were also cited in this chapter.

Loriks' legislative election vote totals were found in "Election Record #2," at the Kingsbury County Courthouse in DeSmet.

Chapter III

The letters, newsletters, newspaper clippings and notes from the Loriks papers are acknowledged in the text. The speeches quoted are on file at South Dakota Farmers Union headquarters in Huron.

The New Deal histories of Link, Karolevitz, Schell, Thompson and Shover, already cited in earlier chapters, again formed much of the background material for the discussion of the South Dakota Farmers Union in the 1930s. A key source for Huey Long is T. Harry Williams' *Huey Long*. John A. Crampton's *The National Farmers Union: Ideology of a Pressure*

Group is an invaluable source of information about the history and politics of the Farmers Union. Additional material about the history and ideology of the Farmers Union was drawn from William P. Tucker's article, "Populist up to Date: the Story of the Farmers Union," that appeared in the October 1947 issue of *Agricultural History*.

The John D. Hicks and Theodore Saloutos book on agricultural discontent, cited in the previous chapter, was also a source of this chapter.

Chapter IV

In addition to conversations with both Emil Loriks and his daughter, Ruth Ann Carlson, most of the description and analysis of the 1938 Congressional campaign comes from South Dakota State University history professor Dr. John Miller's article, "McCarthyism Before McCarthy: the 1938 Election in South Dakota," that appeared in the summer 1982 *Heritage of the Great Plains*. The letters quoted in this chapter are found in the Loriks papers. The 1938 Democratic primary data came from the *1939 South Dakota Legislative Manual* while the breakdown for Kingsbury County was found in "Election Record #2," in the county courthouse at DeSmet. The 1938 national election data came from William E. Leuchtenburg's *Franklin D. Roosevelt and the New Deal, 1932-1940*. The John Miller quotes about Emil Loriks' lack of bitterness were made at meetings October 9 (in Brookings) and October 18, 1984 (Huron) sponsored by the South Dakota Committee on the Humanities that discussed Emil Loriks' public service career. The discussion on Popular Front strategy is drawn both from Leuchtenburg and from Lowell K. Dyson's *Red Harvest*, already cited in Chapter I.

Chapter V

The letters, speech texts and newspaper clippings found in the Loriks papers were cited in the text. Interview sources for this chapter included Robert Handschin and John Barron, whose letters to the author were also cited in the text. Farmers

Union positions were drawn from a pamphlet, "Highlights of Agricultural Progress, Farmers Union," published in 1964 and supplied to the author by Robert Handschin. The Dyson and Crampton books, previously cited, also provided background material for this chapter. Handschin also supplied the author with a memo about the GTA that he had written at the time of its thirtieth anniversary.

Chapter VI

Letters, newspaper clippings and GTA annual reports were found in the Loriks papers, as was the text of the 1964 speech that Emil Loriks delivered to the national Farmers Union convention. Other source materials included the Handschin memo, cited in the previous chapter, and also a pamphlet, "Grain Terminal Association, 1938-1981," supplied to the author by Handschin.

There is no history, scholarly or popular, of the Grain Terminal Association, nor is there a biography of M.W. Thatcher.

Chapter VII

The primary sources in this chapter are letters and newspaper clippings found in the Loriks papers. These materials are directly cited in the text. Interviews with Emil Loriks and Ruth Ann Carlson provided the anecedotal material about the family.

Chapter VIII

The interview sources for this chapter were Emil Loriks; his daughter, Ruth Ann Carlson; and his sister, Emma Turnquist. Loriks' speeches while president of the South Dakota Farmers Union were found in back issues of the *South Dakota Union Farmer*. His presidential addresses to the state Farmers Union conventions were found at Union headquarters in Huron. The GTA annual reports, which contain Loriks' written yearly reports while he was GTA president were found either in his papers, or on file at Harvest States headquarters in St. Paul.

The text of the 1938 NBC speech was found in the Loriks papers as were the notes for the speech given in 1962 at Brady, Montana.

Chapter IX

The William Janklow comments about Emil Loriks were written in a letter to the author on March 8, 1985. Letters and newspaper stories are cited in the text. Interview sources were Robert Handschin, Glenn Levitt, Halvor Stenson and Ben Radcliffe, as well as Emil Loriks and his daughter, Ruth Ann Carlson. The notes for the 1959 telephone cooperative speech were found in the Loriks papers.

Index

Note About The Author

Writer Elizabeth Evenson Williams lives in Brookings, where she is Reading Series Coordinator for the South Dakota Committee on the Humanities and a part-time instructor in journalism and speech at South Dakota State University. A native South Dakotan, Mrs. Williams holds degrees from SDSU and the University of Wisconsin-Madison. Her husband, Louis, is professor of English at SDSU, and daughter, Katie, is a student at Brookings High School.